# QUIT!

How to give up smoking once and for all, and regain control of your health, wealth and happiness — in just 2 weeks!

# Paul Metcalfe

First Printing: 2019

Copyright © 2019 by Paul Metcalfe
All rights reserved.

Printed in the United Kingdom.

All rights reserved. This book or any of its parts may not be reproduced or used in any manner whatsoever without the express written permission of the author and publisher. However, brief quotations are permitted.

Authors and their publications mentioned in this work and bibliography have their copyright protection. All brand and product names used in this book are trademarks, registered trademarks, or trade names and belong to the respective owners.

The author is not associated with any product or vendor in this book.

## Dedication

This book is dedicated to every smoker in the world who really, truly wishes to quit their habit and regain control of their life, health, wealth and happiness, not just for now, but forever. You *can* do it, and with this book I will show you exactly how.

# Contents

| | |
|---|---|
| Introduction | 11 |
| **Session 1: Why Do We Smoke?** | **15** |
| Introduction | 15 |
| What Happens When You Take a Drag? | 19 |
| Why Do We Smoke? | 23 |
| **Session 2: Reasons to Quit** | **37** |
| Your Health | 39 |
| Other People's Health | 43 |
| Stress Levels | 45 |
| Your Appearance | 47 |
| You Will Save a Shedload of Money | 49 |
| Cut Down on Tobacco Company Profits | 52 |
| Women: Conception and Pregnancy | 55 |
| Men: Sexual Problems Can Be Cured! | 57 |
| You'll Get Your Senses of Smell and Taste Back | 58 |
| Final Thoughts | 59 |
| **Introduction to the Hypnotherapy Recording** | **63** |
| **Session 3: Preparing to Quit** | **67** |
| Cutting Down | 68 |
| Nicotine Patches / Nicotine Gum | 70 |
| e-Cigarettes / Vaping | 71 |
| 1. Set a Date | 74 |
| 2. Tell Everyone that You're Quitting | 76 |

3. Anticipate the Problems Ahead .................................. 78
  4. Remove All Cigarettes and Associated Items from Your Environment. ................................................................. 83
  5. Talk to Your Doctor About Quitting ........................... 84

**Session 4: Quitting** ......................................................... 85
  The First 24 Hours ......................................................... 87
  Dealing with it ................................................................ 89
  What to Expect to Start With......................................... 90
  How Should You Feel? ................................................... 92
  Cash .................................................................................. 93
  Recording Your Feelings................................................. 94
  Affirmations .................................................................... 95
  Eating ............................................................................... 98
  Time.................................................................................. 99

**Session 5: Remaining a Non-Smoker** ...................... 103
  Once an Addict, Always an Addict............................... 104
  Trigger Situations ......................................................... 106
  Keeping on the Straight and Narrow........................... 107
  Helping Others to Quit ................................................. 110
  Affirmations .................................................................. 112
  Dealing with Slips, Trips and Backslides ...................... 113

**Session 6: Repairing the Damage** ........................... 115
  Clean Air ........................................................................ 117
  Diet.................................................................................. 124

Foods to Avoid ............................................................. 127

Exercise........................................................................ 132

Cleaning Yellow-Stained Fingers ................................... 136

Cleaning Yellow-Stained Teeth...................................... 136

Finally .......................................................................... 137

**Appendix**...................................................................... 139

One last thing... ............................................................ 140

# Hypnotherapy Tracks Download

This book comes complete with four hypnotherapy track downloads. To obtain your hypnotherapy tracks, visit

https://quitsmokebook.com/hypnosessions

On this website you will be able to download the tracks in .mp3 format, or play them directly from the site.

## Acknowledgements

I would like to acknowledge the assistance of the many health professionals who have helped in the research and preparation of this book, and of the smokers and ex-smokers who have willingly shared their stories of success and failure.

Also to my friend Chris Payne, whose many suggestions immeasurably improved this book, to Toby Payne for the infographics on pages 17 and 41, to Emily Doheny for her fabulous illustrations and to Ken Leeder for last-minute work on the front cover.

I must also add huge thanks to my wonderful wife, Toni, who patiently read the manuscript several times, making many suggestions, all of which have improved this book significantly.

## About the Author

Paul Metcalfe has a mission: to find cures and workarounds for many of life's everyday problems and hardships.

Life can be easier, more pleasant, relaxing, healthy and comfortable. Paul's mission is to find these cures and life-improving strategies and to explain them to as many people as possible.

No fluff, no flannel, no half-baked theories... just solid facts and proven solutions. Life should be enjoyed, not endured.

# Introduction

How to Use This Book to Become a Non-Smoker Forever

*We're going to climb a mountain together*

I'm going to start this book with a surprise: **I don't want you to give up smoking.**

Not straight away, anyway.

Giving up smoking is one of the most important decisions you have ever made, for yourself, your family and your friends. It's important that we get it right.

This will require time and effort on your part, but I'll be with you all the way. Once you start using the hypnotherapy recording, you'll hear my voice every day. I want you to think of me as being by your side every time the craving comes to you (and it will, but don't worry, there are lots of methods in the book to help you to overcome them with relative ease).

Take your time in reading the material. Don't read more than one Session per day. Once you have finished reading a Session, sit back in the quiet and think about what you have just read and how it relates to you.

You should start reading the first Session in the book as soon as you are ready.

If you are short on time and can't get through a whole Session in a day, that doesn't matter, just remember that when you do finish one, don't move on to the next one until the following day.

Once you have read the third Session, read the Introduction to the Hypnotherapy recordings. This is a crucial part of the process, and will be a great help in your journey towards being a permanent non-smoker. The rule about not reading more than one Session per day does not apply to the Hypnotherapy Introduction.

Use the hypnotherapy recording once a day, when you can guarantee not to be disturbed for 30 minutes. If you *absolutely can't* manage 30 minutes, there is a shorter session that you can use.

***Do not be tempted to use this all the time. It won't work nearly as well as the full session.***

There are two shorter sessions included as well. Think of these as emergency measures. They will help to get you over the worst moments of craving.

Shut yourself away from the World, and let everyone who could disturb you know that you absolutely must be left undisturbed for half an hour.

When you have read the Hypnotherapy Introduction, put the book down until the following day and then read Session Four.

Please note that throughout this book, whenever I refer to cigarettes, you may assume that I mean cigar, cigarette, cigarillo, pipe, bong or whatever other method you use to inhale tobacco smoke, or chewing tobacco or snuff.

## Disclaimer

This book does not represent medical advice. Before embarking on any program to quit smoking, you must talk to your doctor or medical professional. In the event of a conflict between their advice and what you read in this book, always follow the advice given by your doctor or medical practitioner.

# 1

## Session 1: Why Do We Smoke?

### Introduction

I want you to read every word of this session. There is much here that you won't want to read. None of it is untrue. It will, I admit, make for uncomfortable reading. You may even feel anger towards me for saying these things. In your heart, however, you will know that I'm right. Hang on to that, because that is your hope. It's the hope that you can kick this damaging habit once and for all. You've made a huge leap by getting this far. Come with me now, and we'll beat this thing together!

If we are truly to get to grips with defeating the addiction to smoking, it's essential that we first examine why it is that we smoke. Finding reasons to smoke provides props for the addiction, reasons why we probably shouldn't give up after all. We need to find these props and knock them down, one by one, until it's clear that we actually have no 'reasons' to smoke at all, only excuses not to give up.

People who smoke can give you a hundred reasons why they smoke and a hundred more why they should quit. So why are there still so many people lighting up? Addiction is the answer to that question. When you take a drag on a cigarette, **hundreds of chemicals** are introduced into your body. The most addictive of those chemicals is nicotine.

Nicotine is a highly addictive drug, just like cocaine, marijuana and heroin, and potentially no less dangerous. When your body is addicted to any drug, removing a constant supply of that drug from your system can cause real difficulty. Your body initially finds it hard to cope without the effect of the drug. This leads to cravings, which can become quite severe. Denying these cravings (which is what you will be doing) leads to withdrawal **symptoms**. Dealing with withdrawal is at the core of any drug rehabilitation program, and a drug rehabilitation program is what you are about to begin. Don't be frightened by the prospect of quitting and what that might entail. All will be well in the end.

But first, we need to stare the beast in the eye. This is the stuff that you should be *really very* frightened of. **Do not skip this**. You **need** to read it. You **need** to know this. You **need** to be frightened by it, and you **need** to know that you can be **free of this!** You **can** stare the beast in the eye and make it back down!

Consider the statistics:

1 out of every 5 deaths in the Western World every year can be directly linked to smoking.

Smoking reduces life expectancy by 7 to 8 years, sometimes **much** more.

Since 1964, over 2,500,000 non-smoking children and adults have died as a result of inhaling second-hand smoke. Just ponder on that for a moment. That's...

## *Two and a half million non-smokers killed by smokers.*

That number could only be equalled by a **major war**.

Smoking is directly responsible for the majority of all cases of cancers of the lung, larynx, trachea, oesophagus, bladder, cervix, pancreas, kidney and bronchus (air passages in the respiratory system).

Smoking has been proved to decrease blood flow, which in men can lead to impotence.

Respiratory illnesses are high amongst smokers. In some cases (many more than in the non-smoking population) this can result in pulmonary illnesses such as chronic obstructive pulmonary disease (COPD) and pneumonia, which are responsible for over 85,000 deaths every year.

Smoking during pregnancy increases the risk of miscarriage and foetal growth retardation. It also causes about 5–6% of prenatal deaths, 17–26% of low-birth-weight births, and 7–10% of pre-term deliveries.

If you smoke, you are:

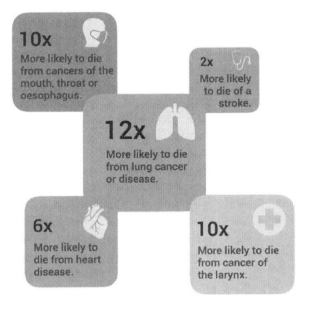

Cigarettes are responsible for about a quarter of all deaths from house fires, causing about a thousand fire-related deaths and 3,500 injuries every year.

Cigarettes contain over 7,000 chemical compounds and hundreds of those are toxic. About 70 of these chemicals are known to be carcinogenic (cancer-inducing). **Seventy** cancer-causing chemicals with every drag!

You are introducing lethal substances into your body every time you take a puff. Smoking is the biggest danger to your health that you can expose yourself to. ***It's like playing chicken with an express train with every puff. One day, maybe later, maybe sooner than you think, the train will win.***

Whenever the beast catches up with you, I absolutely guarantee that you will not be ready for it.

Smoking kills – it's a fact. Tens of thousands of people become seriously ill every year because of smoking – either directly or indirectly. Thousands of children suffer the effects of second-hand smoke from their parents or caregivers. But I don't have to tell you that. You already know. That's why you've taken the ***brave decision to quit***, and it's why you're here, now.

## What Happens When You Take a Drag?

The drugs in tobacco smoke, particularly nicotine, have a profound effect on your body's biochemistry. The results are literally mind-altering. A nicotine dependency will develop very quickly, even if you only smoke a few per day. The level of dependency, it is true, is higher amongst heavy smokers, but even in light smokers, it is very high.

*It's coming – faster than you think*

The effects of the drug are felt within just a few seconds of your initial drag. Nicotine can help you think more clearly if you have the dependency. Without the dependency, of course, you don't need the drug. The dependency (addiction, in other words) causes symptoms of withdrawal to occur fairly rapidly after your last cigarette. The symptoms include increased stress and anxiety, even an almost physical 'jitteriness'. The 'quick fix' is to have another cigarette, flooding your brain and body with the drugs that it is craving. This gives the false impression that cigarettes help you relax. In fact, ***all they do is relieve the symptoms that they themselves cause***.

Nicotine encourages the heightened production of certain hormones within the body. This leads the regular smoker to become additionally addicted to increased hormone levels. Once a cigarette has been finished, the hormone levels begin to drop back towards their normal, healthy values. This in turn adds another level of craving. The smoker feels the need for higher hormone levels, which drives the need to have yet another cigarette.

Almost the moment you light up, the smoke begins to affect your eyes and your respiratory system – your nose and mouth. Through the incendiary action of the cigarette, various noxious gases are produced:

Carbon monoxide (CO): a colourless and odourless but nevertheless highly toxic gas. It reduces the ability of red blood cells to transfer oxygen to vital organs such as the heart, brain, and muscles, and is largely responsible for smokers' inability to perform much exercise without gasping for breath.

Hydrogen cyanide (HCN): yes, that's right – *cyanide*. Cyanide, almost a byword for 'poison', damages the lung's capability to keep itself clean. Your lungs contain small 'hairs' called cilia, which help to clean the lungs. These are damaged by cyanide. Cyanide causes physical weakness, headaches, nausea, vomiting, rapid, shallow breathing and ultimately, of course, death.

Hydrogen sulphide ($H_2S$): this is the gas responsible for the smell of rotten eggs; the lethal concentration of this substance is **even lower** than that for hydrogen cyanide.

Formaldehyde ($CH_2O$): a chemical used for preserving dead tissue in the form of embalming fluid. A known carcinogen.

Ammonia ($CH_4$): the substance responsible for the sharp smell of old, stale urine.

Benzene ($C_6H_6$): a chemical so deadly that use of it outside industrial processes is almost totally banned. It is harmful and cancer-causing at any level of exposure at all.

All these substances – and many more – are produced and are drawn into your mouth, throat, air passages and lungs.

Your **lungs** are put under *immediate* stress. The lungs' ability to self-cleanse is weakened. The 'scrubber cells' that remove foreign particles from the air sacs in your lungs are reduced in effectiveness. The tiny hairs in your lungs that protect them from unwanted particles are damaged and destroyed by the chemicals in cigarette smoke.

The harm caused to your air passages causes you to cough. The more you cough, the more mucus is produced in an attempt to soothe the irritation. The mucus acts as a good breeding-ground for bacteria. This, in turn, makes you more susceptible to colds and other more serious infections. The germs and viruses responsible for flu, bronchitis and other pulmonary diseases will find a happy home here.

Further damage can be caused by long exposure to cigarette smoke. The very tissue which enables your lungs to expand can be damaged, leading to severe diseases such as emphysema and chronic obstructive pulmonary disease (COPD).

Your heart is also put under stress. Due to the pressure put on your lungs, your heart is forced to work harder. Within 10 minutes of lighting up, your heart could be working up to 30% harder than it normally should. This, in turn, leads to an increase in blood pressure. Increased heart rate and blood pressure subject you to an increased risk of stroke and heart attack.

Carbon monoxide (see above) will be drawn into your lungs. The molecules of carbon monoxide attach themselves to haemoglobin in your bloodstream. Haemoglobin is the substance that carries oxygen through your blood from the lungs to the sites within your body where oxygen is needed (tissues, organs). With the receptor sites on the haemoglobin filled with carbon monoxide molecules instead of oxygen molecules, the haemoglobin naturally can carry less life-giving oxygen to your vital organs, such as your brain and heart. Your body will thus become oxygen-starved.

Within seconds of your first drag, the nicotine pulled into your lungs has been absorbed into the bloodstream and transported to your brain. This stimulates your central nervous system, increasing heart rate and blood pressure even more and forcing your heart to demand more oxygen – which it doesn't get because the haemoglobin which should carry the oxygen to your heart is clogged up with carbon monoxide molecules.

The blood vessels in your skin will contract, making your skin age more quickly, and encourage the formation of wrinkles and other signs of premature ageing.

Note how the two aspects of tobacco work together to cause you harm – the most damaging chemicals are contained in the **tar**, but the **nicotine**, in addition to the damage it does by itself, keeps you coming back for more.

## Now, Take a Deep Breath

OK, take a moment. That last section was very unpleasant. But it was also all true. Next time you think of lighting up a cigarette for the temporary relief it gives you, just think back on that previous section. None of this is designed to scare you. It's simply the facts. And frankly, if it *doesn't* scare you, maybe you have more serious problems than smoking!

Apart from a serious reappraisal of your priorities, what I want you to take away from this is that whilst a cigarette may seem to calm and relax you and make you feel generally better about the world and more able to cope, this is **not** in fact true. All that the cigarette will do is ***temporarily relieve you from the cravings caused by the addiction given to you by the cigarettes in the first place***.

Altogether, these effects of smoking and the multiple forms of addiction that it causes produces a tight, vicious circle that is very difficult to break. If you have tried and failed to give up smoking before (as many smokers have – most smokers want to give it up), you will be familiar with the problem. Yes, it is difficult, and this course that you've embarked on *will* be difficult. You are to be applauded for having the bravery to embark on the course.

**BUT** the successful conclusion of this course will bring to you incalculable benefits. These benefits will be discussed in some detail in the next Session. I hope you're excited about them, I know I'm excited about telling you about them. You cannot imagine just how much you will gain from quitting.

For now, though, let's have a look at some of the 'reasons' why we smoke. I hope you'll see after reading the next section that none of these are truly reasons at all. At best, they are merely excuses for behaviour that is both self-destructive and seriously damaging to everyone else.

## Why Do We Smoke?

Firstly, let's look at the reasons why anybody begins smoking in the first place. From the point of view of a non-smoker, smoking would appear to have no advantages and an almost countless number of disadvantages. Yet we were all non-smokers at one time. After all, nobody is born a smoker, and still many people end up smoking despite the obvious disadvantages of smoking. Why?

For the vast majority of smokers, it will have been peer pressure during teenage years that resulted in them becoming smokers.

'Those kids look so cool round the back of the bike shed with their fags and shifty eyes.'

During our teenage years, we desperately want to conform, to look 'good', to be in with the in-crowd, to attain, somehow, some small measure of superiority over our peers. It is a dangerous time, and it's the time when we take on board most of the bad habits, bad attitudes and bad ideologies that will drag us down for the rest of our lives.

We can't deal with all our life issues here, but we can address the one bad habit that led to you buying this book.

Think back to the time when you had your first cigarette. Did it make you feel special? Part of a special group? Did it make you feel older? Did you feel that it was a decision that you had come to by yourself, perhaps in the face of parental opposition? It probably made you feel more adult. Big. Clever.

All these thoughts are perfectly understandable in a teenager. After all, how often have you thought 'If only I knew then what I know now'? Let's face it – how much does a teenager actually know, despite their constant rants of how 'you don't understand!'?

Yeah, think about it. ***Teenagers know balls all about anything***.

'It makes me look cool.' No. It makes you look like an idiot.

Sometimes, an adult can take up smoking even if they have never smoked as a young, easily influenced teenager. Again, the cause of this is almost always peer pressure. Maybe you went from school into a working environment where most of your workmates smoked, in the days before the blanket ban on workplace smoking. In order to 'fit in' with your new pals, to feel more part of the team, you accepted one or two fags from them. Eventually, you were taking every fag offered. Then, of course, you feel pressure not to be the one always taking cigarettes, so you buy a pack – just to offer around, of course. Then you buy another. The beast has sunk its claws into you.

What you should take away from this discussion is that it's *not your fault!* It's social pressure and brilliant marketing that gets you started and the nicotine that keeps you hooked!

Let's have an objective look at some of the many excuses (we can't talk of *reasons* because there is no reason involved by this stage) that smokers give when asked why they smoke, or why they haven't quit. These are the **six commonest excuses** for not giving up smoking:

### 1. 'I Like the Taste / I Enjoy Smoking.'

OK, let's address the subject of taste. One of the most obvious effects of smoking, especially over a long period of time, is that of reduced senses of both smell and taste. When you had your first cigarette – when your taste buds were still working – did you think 'Oh, wow! This tastes so good!'?

No, you didn't, your thoughts were probably more along the lines of 'Urgh! This is foul! How can anyone do this? Still, better keep going – don't want to look soft.'

Just think for a moment if you had thought 'Urgh! This is foul! How can anyone do this?' Then you spat the thing out, never to touch one again. By now, how much would the scorn of your playground friends matter?

Ask almost any smoker why they continue to indulge in such a dangerous habit and they will normally reply, 'Because I like smoking.' While they may say this in all honesty, it is a very misleading statement, both to the listener and to the smoker him or herself. They do not smoke because they enjoy smoking; rather they smoke because they do not enjoy **not smoking** and that is a very different thing.

Nicotine is a powerfully addictive drug. The smoker is in a constant battle to maintain a narrow range of nicotine in their bloodstream (known technically as the 'serum nicotine level'). Every time the smoker's serum nicotine level falls below the minimum limit, they experience drug withdrawal.

They become tense, irritable, anxious, and, in some cases, even show physical symptoms. Obviously, these feelings are not enjoyable. The only thing that will alleviate these acute symptoms will be a cigarette. The nicotine withdrawal is removed by another influx of the drug and the smoker feels better. The obvious – *though wrong* – conclusion is that they enjoyed smoking the cigarette.

A smoker must also be cautious not to exceed their upper limit of tolerance for nicotine or else they will suffer varying degrees of nicotine poisoning. Many smokers can attest to this condition.

It usually occurs after parties or extremely tense situations when the smoker finds him or herself exceeding their normal level of consumption. They feel sick, nauseous, dizzy and generally miserable.

Being a smoker is a delicate balancing act. You have to work hard to keep the balance between having too much or too little nicotine in your bloodstream. One leads to withdrawal, the other to poisoning.

The fear which accompanies initial smoking cessation is that the rest of the ex-smoker's entire life will be as horrible as the first few days without cigarettes. What ex-smokers will learn is that within a short period of time, the physical withdrawal will start to diminish.

First, the urges will weaken in intensity and then become shorter in duration. There will be longer time intervals between urges. It will eventually reach the point where the ex-smoker will desire a cigarette very infrequently, if ever. Those who continue to smoke will continue to be in a constant battle of maintaining their serum nicotine level.

## 2. 'It Helps Me Relax / I Have a Very Stressful Job / Life'

This again comes down to the cyclic nature of nicotine addiction. Maybe a cigarette does give you the impression that you relax. Yes, maybe you do relax, but why do you need to relax?

Most times, it is the addiction itself that causes the stress. Yes, I know we keep coming back to this, but it is **absolutely vital** that you understand this totally.

To a smoker, a cigarette is very much like an infant's comfort blanket. It's a crutch that we use when we don't want to face a situation. Feel pressured at work? You have a smoke. Stressed out at home? You have a smoke. Money problems? Relationship problems? Health problems? Smoke and you won't feel so stressed about it.

The fact is, as long as anyone continues to develop physically, emotionally, intellectually, professionally or spiritually, they too will experience growing pains. Adults are prone to hurt, pain, sadness, depression and anxieties just as children are.

These feelings are all necessary if we wish to continue to develop our minds and bodies. Without such growth, we would not experience happiness, satisfaction, contentment or purpose to their full extent.

Stress has a physiological effect on the body which makes the urine acidic. Whenever the urine becomes acidic, the body excretes nicotine at an accelerated rate. Thus, when a smoker encounters a stressful situation, they lose nicotine and go into drug withdrawal faster than at less stressful times.

Smoking because you're stressed **only adds more stress**. You feel more pressure for taking part in an activity that you know is bad for you but you are unable to stop. When you smoke due to excessive stress, you are transferring blame elsewhere instead of attributing it where it belongs – with your addiction.

When you are stressed out, your body will react in normal ways. When you use a cigarette to alleviate that reaction, you're just creating other reactions that will have to be addressed eventually as well.

**Smoking can't solve *any* problem in life**. No matter what the problem, there are always other, much better ways to help yourself besides picking up a cigarette.

## 3. 'I'm Only a Social Smoker.'

'I'm not addicted, I just smoke to be sociable.' Sorry, but nicotine is **so** addictive that even a few cigarettes will be enough for the beast to get its claws into you. If you truly are just a social smoker, don't smoke next time you're with your smoking friends. Just don't do it.

Smoking 'socially' can be how it starts for some, just like the example I gave above about smoking because your workmates smoke. You're having drinks with friends and one of them smokes. You have a puff because the alcohol has numbed your sensibility. Pretty soon, you're cadging cigarettes off anyone you can find. Then you buy your first pack. Peer pressure drives you into the claws of the beast.

You **think** that you're enjoying smoking the cigarette, but what you are *actually* enjoying is the good company of your friends and the sociability of the situation. We human beings make very strong associations in our minds. If we regularly enjoy ourselves in the company of friends, and smoke at the same time, we associate the good feelings with smoking. It's totally wrong, but we all make poor associations. Think about things that make you feel good or bad. Separate what it is about a situation that really makes you feel good or bad, and what is just secondary. I'm sure you'll find much to think about.

Now that smoking is banned in all places such as pubs, restaurants, cinemas etc., of course, you now have to *remove yourself* from the very company that you enjoy in order to satisfy your cravings, which are most definitely not what is making the event pleasant and enjoyable. Go and stand outside for a bit in the cold, wind and rain. There's real pleasure!

Of course, you keep telling yourself that you only smoke when you socialise. This is where the problem comes in. Because you have convinced yourself of this, you begin drinking just so you can have a smoke. Now you're not only damaging your body with nicotine, but you can end up drinking too much in order to satisfy your nicotine cravings!

And, yes, we're back at this same cyclic point again. At least by now you should be getting an idea of how important it is.

### 4. 'If I quit, I'll pile on the pounds.'

Alright, let's face this one. This one is (if you'll pardon the pun) something of a 'biggy' when it comes to excuses not to quit smoking. I'm sure we've all seen people we know, even friends, who have successfully given up smoking and who then balloon to previously unimagined vastness. Why does this happen? Does smoking keep you slim and trim? No, of course not, we've all seen overweight smokers.

What happens is that the quitter adopts a substitute behaviour for his or her smoking habit. Many smokers turn to eating sweets as a substitute behaviour. In effect, what they've done is to swap one bad habit for another. I've seen quitters shovelling sweets into their mouths like there was no tomorrow. It's as if they always have to have something in their mouth to distract them from the fact that there isn't a cigarette there.

It's not the best road to take, not by a long way. Sugar has finally been revealed as one of the great evils of the food industry today. Its effects lead to obesity, ill health and diseases such as type 2 diabetes. Come on, you're abandoning one bad lifestyle choice, don't simply take up another one instead!

These days there are many zero- and low-sugar alternatives. If sucking on a sweet will help you, then by all means do that – **but go for the sugar-free option every time!**

Another alternative, favoured by quitters for many years, is the veggie-sticks option. Whenever you feel the need for a cigarette, or simply to do something with your hands and mouth (old habits die hard), reach for a carrot or celery stick. Not only will the veggie-stick not do you any harm, it will actually do you good! Imagine that!

## 5. 'I'm addicted – there's nothing I can do about it / I've smoked for years – it's too late to stop now.'

Oh yes? What are you reading this for then? The truth is that there is **always** something you can do about it, and it is **never** too late.

This course will take you by the hand and demonstrate in the best way possible that there **is** something you can do about it and it's **NOT** too late. What's the best way? ***By getting you off your addiction quickly and forever!***

The simple fact is that addictions **can** be beaten, and **are** being beaten every day. There are worse addictions than nicotine. Every day, addicts to drugs such as cocaine and heroin are successfully beating their addictions and rejoining society. If they can beat their terrible addictions, ***then you can beat yours***. Being a nicotine addict doesn't make you a social outcast. OK, you are becoming one more and more as the law forces you outside and away from the 'society' that remains indoors in the office, pub, restaurant, cafe, cinema – in fact, any enclosed space. Technically, you can't even smoke in a bus shelter! But come on – you're not exactly a heroin addict, are you? If **heroin addicts** can beat their addiction, then ***I'm damned sure you can beat your much lesser one***.

Saying that you're addicted and there's nothing you can do about it is just feeble wimping out. **Of course** you can do something about it and I'm determined that together we can beat this thing once and for all.

## 6. 'Smokers are cool / have more fun / look great / look sexy'

Alright, let's have a good, hard look at this one. Spoiler alert! Here's what we're going to conclude:

Smokers are cool – er, no they're not.

Smokers have more fun – no they don't.

Smokers look great – I'm starting to laugh.

Smokers look sexy – Stop it! I'm on the floor, rolling with laughter!

One thing we all have to cope with is the images that bombard us every day from television, cinema, billboards, the internet and our peer group.

Although advertising on television, cinema and billboards is now banned, it is still common to see actors smoking, attempting to look 'cool'.

Fortunately, thanks to the advertising ban, we no longer have to deal with the ridiculous adverts that projected an image of the cool, sexy smoker. Just think 'Marlboro Man' and you'll know what I mean.

The reality is so different it just isn't funny.

Imagine the situation: you're at a party, and across the room, you spy the object of your desire. She or he is chatting with somebody you don't know. Now's the time to make your move. Perhaps you laugh a little louder at a joke one of your friends has just made, maybe you can attract their attention that way. Your desired one looks up. They look over towards you. It worked! Look at your love interest! There's just the trace of a smile, the eyes are narrowing in just *that* way! Time to move to the next level.

You casually pull a cigarette out of the pack. You tap it to settle the tobacco, like a professional smoker. You raise it to your lips, and bring the lighter up, sparking it. The tiny flame erupts and you bring it to the tip of the cigarette. How cool are you? You draw in the smoke, lighting the cigarette. You breathe in deeply, pulling the cigarette from your lips and looking appreciatively at it as you blow that first billow of cool, sexy smoke towards the ceiling.

You look past your sex-aid towards the one you fancy. Oh yes! You are so attractive right now! That super cool ciggie-lighting manoeuvre has tipped the balance in your favour. Time to saunter across the room and nail the deal.

Meanwhile, the object of your desire has just glanced across the room. He or she sees you. You look alright, maybe there's a tiny flutter of interest. What's that you're doing? Is that a cigarette? Oh, dear God! They're trying to be cool by lighting a fag! The prospects flash through your object of desire's mind. This is someone who thinks that they're cool. Here's someone who is going to stink to high heaven. Kissing that ashtray mouth would make me sick!

More thoughts flash across their mind. Look – this is a person who cares nothing for their own health, even their own life. Even worse, they couldn't give a hoot about anyone else's health or life! That cigarette may be the one that gives someone in this room terminal cancer, and look at them! They couldn't give a damn whether they kill anyone else or not!

Their clothes will stink. Their house will stink. All their possessions will stink. What an inconsiderate loser!

### *How do you think your next move will go?*

Smokers care nothing for their own health.

Smokers care nothing for their own life.

Smokers care nothing for anyone else's health.

Smokers care nothing for anyone else's life. Remember – since 1964, **smokers have killed two and a half million non-smokers**. I'm not making this stuff up – *this is real*!

Smokers stink.

Smokers' houses stink.

Smokers' possessions stink.

Smokers are as far from cool and sexy as it is possible to get.

And that is why **you** have decided to quit. You know all the above to be true, and you have decided to do something about it. Already, you are starting to think and behave like a non-smoker.

That means that I can help you. It means there is real hope for you. It means that quitting is a realistic and achievable goal for you!

**WHAT SMOKERS THINK THEY LOOK LIKE**  **WHAT EVERYONE ELSE SEES**

Some smokers say they smoke because they are nervous. Others say they smoke to celebrate. Some think they smoke for energy. Many smoke to 'look sexy'. Yet others smoke to stay awake or to sleep. Some think they smoke to think.

None of these reasons satisfactorily explain why people continue smoking. However, the answer is, in fact, quite simple. Smokers smoke cigarettes because they are smokers. More precisely, smokers smoke cigarettes because they are smoke addicts, in the same way that alcoholics are alcohol addicts.

A smoke addict, like any other drug addict, has become hooked on a chemical substance. In the cigarette smoker's case, nicotine is the culprit. They are at the point where the failure to maintain a minimum level of nicotine in the bloodstream leads to the **nicotine abstinence syndrome**, a form of drug withdrawal. Anything that makes them lose nicotine makes them smoke.

Most smokers feel that when they are nervous or upset, cigarettes help calm them down. The calming effect, however, is not relief from the emotional strain of the situation, but actually the effect of replenishing the nicotine supply and temporarily ending the withdrawal.

It is easy to understand why the smoker without this basic knowledge of stress and its nicotine effect is afraid to give up smoking. ***They feel that they will be giving up a very effective stress management technique***. But once they give up smoking for a short period of time, they will become calmer, even under stress, than when they were smokers.

The explanation of how physiological changes in the body make them smoke is difficult for some smokers to believe. But nearly all smokers can easily relate to other situations which also alter the excretion rate of nicotine.

Ask a smoker what happens to his or her smoking consumption after drinking alcohol, and you can be sure he or she will answer that it goes up. If asked how much their consumption rises, they will normally reply that it doubles or even triples when drinking.

They are usually convinced that this happens because everyone around them is smoking. But if he or she thinks back to a time when they were the only smoker in the room, they will realize that drinking still caused them to smoke more.

Alcohol consumption results in one of the same physiological effect as stress – acidification of the urine. The nicotine level drops dramatically, and the smoker must light one cigarette after another or suffer drug withdrawal.

It is important for you as a smoker considering quitting to understand these concepts because once you *truly understand* why you smoke you will be able more fully to appreciate how **much more simple** life will become as an ex-smoker.

Once you stop smoking, the nicotine will begin to leave your body, and **within two weeks all the nicotine will be gone**. Once the nicotine is totally out of your body, the effects of the withdrawal will quickly begin to diminish. No longer will you experience drug withdrawal states whenever encountering stress, drinking, or just going too long without smoking.

***In short, you will soon realise that all the benefits you thought you derived from smoking were false effects***. You will realise that you did not need to smoke to deal with stress, or to socialise, or to work. Everything done as a smoker can be done as a non-smoker, and in most cases, these activities can be done more efficiently and make you feel better during them.

As an ex-smoker, you will become a more independent person. It is a good feeling and a major accomplishment to break free from this addiction. But no matter how long you are off smoking and how confident you feel, you must always remember that you are a smoke addict.

It is true that very many ex-smokers become ardent anti-smokers, and nearly all of them will never touch a cigarette again, or even want to. But if you let yourself have another cigarette one day, just for old times' sake, or just to stand out in the sleet and rain with your old smoking buddies, you're setting yourself up for a fall. The addiction can come back very quickly indeed, and the beast will have you trapped once again.

Remember that your 'old smoking friends' will still be your friends, even if you don't join them outside for a quick death-stick. They'll be back in a couple of minutes, maybe coughing a bit. You'll notice the terrible stench they bring back with them…

...and that will be the time when you can start to help *them*. More on this later.

That's all for this session. It hasn't been pleasant, but I hope you'll agree that it is absolutely necessary for you to understand the nature of the beast that has you trapped. The best way to defeat it is to understand it, and understand exactly what is happening to your body as you work your way through the withdrawal symptoms.

In the next session (and please remember not to start reading Session Two until tomorrow), we'll be looking at reasons to quit smoking. I'm sure you have your own reasons, but maybe I can put a few more in front of you. It may even strengthen your resolve.

# 2

## Session 2: Reasons to Quit

Welcome to our second session. I hope you've been thinking about what we discussed in the last session, and that you now have a clearer idea of why you feel the need to keep smoking.

In this session, we're going to look at some really good reasons to quit smoking. In order to come to the decision to quit smoking, as you have already, I'm sure you have thought long and hard about this already, and that you have found one (or many) good reasons to quit.

Even if you do have your own very good reasons for quitting smoking, I still want you to read on. This session may well bring some issues to light that you may not have thought of. This should give you even more reasons to quit, and make you even more sure that you have made the right decision.

It is ***vitally important*** that you have good, solid reasons to quit smoking. Trials have shown that quitters without well thought-out reasons to stop are not as successful as those who have thought long about it and have come up with strong reasons to quit.

Simply being aware of your own reasons will improve your chances of quitting, and staying smoke-free forever.

Let's just list some of the reasons you may have thought of:

1. Health.

The obvious first thought. We've already covered the terrifying range of ways in which smoking is likely to kill you. We won't be going over those again, but we will look at some of the advantages that **NOT** smoking will have on your health.

2. Other People's Health.

This is very important. Those people who are closest to you are in considerable danger from your smoking. You don't want that – of course you don't – but it remains true. We'll have a look at the dangers of secondary smoking.

3. Your Stress Levels Will Decrease.

It's true, much of the stress that you feel now is a result of your nicotine addiction. Once you've kicked that, your stress levels and anxiety will noticeably decrease and you'll become a far calmer and steadier individual.

4. Your Appearance Will Improve.

Smoking has a very detrimental effect on your appearance. Yellow-brown fingers, stained fingernails, brown teeth and gums, prematurely aged skin, wrinkles, spots – all these come from the cigarettes. Another factor is what you smell like. It doesn't matter how much perfume or aftershave you splash on, there's no disguising the stench of a smoker. Be done with that.

5. You Will Save a Shedload of Cash.

We'll be looking at this in some detail. This can be and should be a huge motivator for quitting and also for remaining on the straight and narrow after you have successfully quit.

6. You Can Stick Two Fingers Up at Tobacco Executives.

The Fat Cats in tobacco companies are making a fortune out of ill-health and death. If anyone deserves to lose their jobs it's these bastards. You'll have the pleasure of knowing that at least they won't profit from *your* terminal illness.

7. Women: If You Are Pregnant or Trying to Conceive.

Smoking has a detrimental effect on your ability to conceive. It can also have a devastating effect on an unborn baby. If you are trying to conceive or are already pregnant, you **must** give up smoking.

8. Men: Sexual Problems can be Cured.

Sorry to tell you this chaps, but smoking can have a withering effect on your old chap. Nicotine addiction can lead to impotence and reduced sperm count. Your sexual health is in serious danger whilst you smoke. Now, we don't want that, do we?

9. You'll Get Your Senses of Smell and Taste Back.

This will happen faster than you think. You'll be astonished at how much flavour you've been missing out on for all these years!

Now, go over the above list again and see which of the reasons resonate with you. Think for a few moments how each reason will have a profound effect on **your** life.

It can be a useful exercise to go over this list regularly – at least once a week – to reinforce in your own mind just why it is that you're quitting. This will really help you to keep your eye on the ball and improve your chances of success.

## Your Health

It's absolutely fine to put your health first, even before the health of others. With regard to smoking, it hardly matters anyway, because when you quit you are not only going to make huge improvements in your own health but automatically improve the health of all those around you at the same time.

We've spoken about the risks of all the horrible diseases and noxious chemicals, but now let's look at the ***benefits of quitting*** for your health.

You may be concerned that your health is already too badly damaged. This will be true only in extreme cases where an unwelcome diagnosis has already been made. Most quitters recover their health very well, and it happens **a lot quicker than you think.**

Although, as we all know, smoking does terrible harm to your body, the human body has a remarkable ability to heal itself, even of some of the worst abuses we put it through.

Let's look at a timeline. Have a look at the graphic on the next page, then come back and get more details.

This is what will happen to your body after you quit smoking:

**20 minutes** after you stop smoking, your blood pressure and heart rate will decrease. That's right – the benefits of quitting begin just a few minutes after you stub out your final ciggie. Smokers' blood pressure and heart rates are not permanently elevated, unless they smoke more than one cigarette every 20 minutes, of course. Continually elevating your blood pressure will ultimately have serious effects on your body, but once that final cigarette is consigned to history, your blood pressure will decrease and you will have begun to heal already.

**12 hours** after you quit smoking, the levels of carbon dioxide in your blood will return to normal levels. This means that more oxygen is being processed by your lungs and is being sent via the bloodstream to your vital organs. This is good, right?

**3 days** after quitting, the tension eases in your bronchial tubes, and they relax, allowing you to breathe more freely.

**14 days** after you quit smoking, you will experience an increase in circulation and an improvement in lung function. Oxygen levels are returning to normal. Your heart is starting to recover, as is your liver, kidneys, brain and all the other organs.

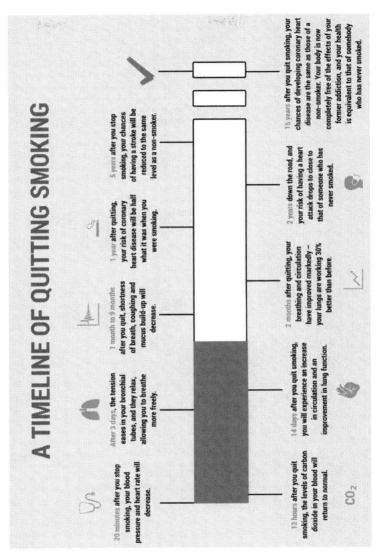

By the way, once you get to 14 days smoke-free, almost all your cravings will be gone. Think about that – you only have

41

to battle with the withdrawal symptoms for two rotten weeks. YOU CAN DO THAT!

**1 month to 9 months** after you quit, shortness of breath, coughing and mucus build-up will decrease. Remember those little hairs in the lungs that we talked about in Session 1? The ones that are damaged by the hydrogen cyanide in cigarette smoke? These are now recovering and beginning to work as they should. The 'scrubber' cells, called 'scavengers' also return to their proper efficiency.

**2 months** after quitting, your breathing and circulation have improved markedly – your lungs are working 30% better than they were when you smoked. You are finding it easier to walk.

**1 year** after quitting, your risk of coronary heart disease will be **half** what it was when you were smoking. It may take this long for your tiredness, shortness of breath and coughing to stop completely, but it could take a lot less.

**2 years** down the road, and your risk of having a heart attack drops to close to that of someone who has never smoked. By now you are so much fitter and healthier than you were just two short years ago. The changes have been dramatic.

**5 years** after you stop smoking, **your chances of having a stroke will be reduced to the same level as a non-smoker.** Your risk of getting lung cancer has halved, and the chances of developing the other cancers associated with smoking have **dramatically reduced**.

**15 years** after you quit smoking, your chances of developing coronary heart disease are the same as those of a non-smoker. Your body is now completely free of the effects of your former addiction, and your health is equivalent to that of somebody who has never smoked.

Now 15 years might seem like a long time at this point, but remember that the worst is over by the end of two weeks. If you never smoke again, your body will continue to repair itself from the damage you have done to it. It will do this quietly and without your being aware of it. Apart, that is, from the odd wonderful moment when you realise that you can now do something that you couldn't do before you stopped smoking.

## Other People's Health

When you think of giving up smoking, think also of the effect that your decision will have on your friends and family – all your loved ones. They will be delighted. Not only will your health improve, theirs will as well.

These days, most smokers who live with non-smokers do have the courtesy to smoke outside the house, and in those situations, the people you live with will have been recovering since you made that correct decision.

The effects of second-hand smoke are no less devastating than those of direct inhalation. 'Passive smoking' as it is called, resulted in the deaths of over two and a half million non-smokers between 1964 and 2014.

Think about it. When you smoke a cigarette, the smoke doesn't all go into your lungs. The tip smokes, filling the atmosphere with all the same deadly chemicals that you pull into yourself – **unfiltered**! Not only that, but once you've finished with your lungful of poisons, you blow it out, subjecting everyone around you to the same lethal cocktail.

It has been clearly demonstrated that constant exposure to second-hand smoke is **even more dangerous** than direct smoking.

In the short-term, exposure to second-hand smoke causes irritation to the eyes and mucous membranes, resulting in coughs, sore throats, headaches, dizziness and nausea.

The longer-term effects are the same as those of smoking. Among non-smokers who live in an atmosphere of continuous exposure to second-hand smoke, the risk of developing lung cancer is three times that of a non-smoker who lives in a clean atmosphere.

Non-smokers who live or work in a smoky atmosphere are **at least** 80% more likely to suffer from a stroke.

Exposure to second-hand smoke also causes serious cardiovascular problems, leading to pulmonary diseases, atherosclerosis, hardened arteries and cardiac arrest. Non-smokers exposed to second-hand smoke are twice as likely to suffer heart attacks.

Studies have also shown that passive smoking increases the risk of a non-smoker developing asthma by up to five times, and for those who already suffer from asthma, second-hand smoke can seriously reduce their lung capacities and function.

Children who are exposed to smoke in their homes are much likelier to suffer from asthma, bronchitis, pneumonia and other respiratory diseases.

It should go without saying that kids exposed to smoking at home are far more likely to take up smoking themselves.

Finally in this section; spare a thought for your poor pets. Cats and dogs in households where one or more residents smoke are far more likely to develop fatal illnesses than those that live in a smoke-free home. It has been estimated that dogs and cats that live in a smoker's house for over a year are 60% more likely to get lung cancer and/or canine and feline lymphoma than their luckier cousins who live in a non-smoker's house.

This has been another scary section, but I don't apologise for it. You need to know this stuff and you need to know what your smoking is doing to other people around you. Face up to the pain and suffering you are causing and *give a damn*!

## Stress Levels

Many smokers believe that smoking is a way of relieving stress, of somehow making life a little easier. In a way, they are right, smoking does reduce stress.

However, the only stress that lighting a cigarette reduces is the stress of the smoker's nicotine addiction screaming out for a hit.

Smokers become more stressed than non-smokers because they are **putting their body under greater stress** by needing to satisfy their addiction almost constantly.

If your workload is stressing you at say 3 out of 10 on the 'anxiety scale', then the craving for nicotine will be adding another 4 or 5 points, taking your stress levels up to 7 or 8 out of 10. Yes, you are stressed, and the cigarette will remove that stress – but it's not the stress of work that it's relieving, it's just the stress of your dependence.

Now, just imagine how it would be if the craving for nicotine wasn't there. Yes, of course there will still be stresses and anxieties during the day – that's just life. Your stress levels will remain much lower, however, because the totally unnecessary additional levels of stress that you're slathering on yourself won't be there.

**Smoking does not relieve the stresses of everyday life, it only relieves the stresses of smoking itself.**

Without the smoke, you will be able to cope much better, once you're over the initial withdrawal period.

***REMEMBER*: that phase will last only a couple of weeks!**

Think also of the other, minor stresses and concerns that giving up smoking will relieve:

- You'll never worry again that you're running out of cigarettes.

- You'll never worry again about finding a spot where you are permitted to smoke.

- You'll never worry again about getting cold and wet whilst you smoke.

- You'll never again worry about keeping enough spare cash on you to be able to buy a packet of cigarettes.

- You'll never have to worry again about being able to find somewhere that will actually sell you a packet of cigarettes.

- You'll never get that sinking feeling in your stomach when the landlord of the pub you're in tells you that they don't sell cigarettes.

- You'll never worry again about the smell of your clothing, especially in intimate circumstances.

- You'll never worry again about your brown teeth and gums.

- You'll never worry again about your atrocious breath.

- You won't need to carry a pack of mints about with you 'just in case'. (Quick tip here – they don't work anyway. Smoker's breath cuts right through even the most powerful mints, and they do nothing for the smell of your clothes).

- You will never again be embarrassed by your yellowed fingers and dirty-looking nails when being introduced to someone for the first time. You can shake their hand with confidence.

**Just think how much easier and less complicated your life is going to be!**

## Your Appearance

I hope by now that you're a long way from believing that smokers look cool and sexy. Only smokers think that. From the point of view of the non-smoker, smokers just look ***terrible***!

There's the obvious staining: brown teeth, brown gums, yellow fingers, dirty fingernails. All this can be gone within a few days of quitting. The teeth may require a visit to the dentist, but that's nothing to worry about. The dentist *can* hurt you – but she won't. Once you've stopped smoking, you won't need another cleaning by the dentist for *years*.

Smoking also has detrimental effects on your skin. Smoking clogs the skin's pores. Reduced oxygen supply and the damaging of blood vessels near the surface of the skin leads to a thinning and weakening of the skin tissue itself. This, in turn, causes wrinkling, poor skin tone and premature ageing. Skin conditions such as acne, rashes and psoriasis flourish under these conditions. Although this might seem a minor point, there is no doubt that the skin of a smoker has little of the 'natural glow' we associate with healthy individuals. The skin of a smoker is dull, grey and unhealthy-looking. ***You can get your glow back***.

Once you stop smoking, some of the damage can be undone, and we'll come on to damage repair in a later session. For now, though, just think how much better you're going to look now that you've taken the brave decision to kick the habit.

As a smoker, you may have noticed that your hair has become thinner and more brittle. Smokers' hair also greys sooner than non-smokers' hair. Amongst men, smokers are about twice as likely to lose their hair than non-smokers.

Again, some of this damage can be undone, and healing starts as soon as you stop smoking.

I'm sorry to say this, but overwhelmingly the worst part of your 'presence' as a smoker is the way you smell. Your own sense of taste and smell have been degraded significantly by the continued inhalation of smoke, so you probably don't even notice it, but your friends, family and everyone you stand near will. Your clothes, hair and even your skin stink.

All this can be fixed. Once you quit, and your clothes have been through the washer, all those nasty smells will become a thing of the past. It will take a couple of weeks for all the toxins to be flushed away from your skin, but we'll soon have you coming up smelling of roses!

# You Will Save a Shedload of Money

That's a phrase you hear a lot these days. Usually, it's some advertiser telling you that you will 'save money' by buying x, y or z. The tiniest moment's thought shows what a fabrication this is. You'd actually 'save' money by not buying that product at all.

The proviso is always 'Ah, yes, what we mean is that if you buy our product, you would potentially save money by not buying the more expensive alternative, sold by our competitors.'

Obviously, what they mean is 'spend less' rather than 'save', but you're still spending, not saving.

You can only save money by not spending money.

Now the obvious question: How much do you spend on cigarettes? You probably hardly notice, it goes in dribs and drabs, a packet here, a packet there.

At the time of writing (2018), a packet of 20 cigarettes from a supermarket costs an average of about £12. That's 60p per cigarette.

How many cigarettes do you smoke in a day? You need to be ***absolutely honest*** with yourself here. You're not telling *me*, you're not admitting it to *anyone else*. Only *you* need to know, but you **do need to know**.

A 'light smoker' – by definition, someone who smokes fewer than 10 cigarettes per day – will therefore be spending between 60p and £5.40 per day on cigarettes. Yeah, easy come, easy go, but in round numbers that's **£200 – £2,000** per year!

An 'average smoker' (and statistically, this is most likely the range you fall into) is one who smokes 10 – 19 cigarettes per day. Between half a pack and a pack a day. That's £6 – £12 per day, or **£2,190 – £4,161** per year.

If you are a 'heavy smoker', that's anything over 20 cigarettes per day, then you're spending **at least £4,380 per year on cigarettes!**

Take a look at this table:

| Cigs per day | Cost per year |
|---|---|
| 1 | £219 |
| 5 | £1,095 |
| 10 | £2,190 |
| 20 | £4,380 |
| 30 | £6,570 |
| 40 | £8,760 |
| 50 | £10,950 |

I hope that's shocked you. It certainly shocked me when I worked it out. Even if you only smoke one cigarette a day, you're burning **over two hundred quid a year!**

A 'modest' ten a day habit is costing you **over two grand!**

If you know exactly how many cigarettes you smoke per day, and your daily count isn't up there on that table, you can work out your annual cost in pounds by using this simple formula:

Cost per year (£) = cigarettes smoked per day x 219

(If you're interested, the 219 comes from 365×0.6, which is the cost per day per cigarette, each cigarette being 60p, or £0.6.)

Work out your annual cost and then I want you to stop reading for a little while. Sit back and close your eyes. Think about that annual figure. Imagine that amount of money being passed to you in a wad of crisp, new banknotes. Just think what you could do with that money. It could go towards a holiday, a new car, the work that really needs doing around the house. If your figure is at the higher end, you could have a cruise, the holiday of a lifetime! **EVERY YEAR!**

What do you need to spend a wodge of cash on right now? What would you like to spend it on? Just sit back now and allow your imagination to run wild. Don't hold back. That's a lot of money there to do with as you wish. Close your eyes now.

Alright? Back to Earth now. Now imagine yourself holding that wad of cash and meekly handing it over to two blank-faced people. They take your money and split it between them. In return, they give you a fatal disease and pour toxic filth over your family. Then they walk away without a backward glance, one to the tobacco company boardroom, the other to the Treasury.

You should be angry by now. It's an appropriate reaction. Dammit, *I'm* angry, and it's *your* money and *your* life!

## Cut Down on Tobacco Company Profits

It is estimated by the American Cancer Society (who publish a very informative web page at https://tobaccoatlas.org) that the global tobacco industry makes profits of over **$35 billion per year**. In round numbers, that's about **£1,000 per second**. That's every second of every day. **Profits**, not **turnover**. Can you even *imagine* that? I can't.

The cost of that obscene profit is **over 6 million deaths per year**. During the whole of the First World War (1914 – 1918), the allied powers lost **4.8 million** soldiers. Tobacco kills more than this *every year.*

Does it seem right to you that the fat cats in tobacco companies are growing rich beyond the dreams of avarice, riding on the backs of 6 million deaths a year?

Would you be happy being in that position? Would you be able to live with yourself knowing the vast cost in human lives that your luxurious lifestyle was costing?

No. Of course you wouldn't. You're not like that. I'm sorry for even asking the question.

Unfortunately, there are enough moral-free, guilt-free, conscience-free people in the world to keep the industry going, and increasing its profits year on year.

Do you want to support their lifestyle? I'm sure you don't, especially when you consider that your death may be just another one of the six million for them not to worry about, or even notice.

Think about this when you're smoking. That coffin nail in your hand is exactly that to you, but to the greedy psychopath on the board of the tobacco company, it's just another enforced donation towards yet another yacht, or private plane, or football club that they choose to buy with your money, your health, your life.

What about the Government? What about all that tax you pay on your cigarettes? Currently, about 64% of the price of a packet of cigarettes is tax. That's about £7.68 on a £12 pack. The Government claims that this is to discourage smoking and to cut down on the number of people smoking and getting ill and dying.

Lies.

If the Government really wanted to cut down on smoking and all its effects, they'd put the price of a packet of cigarettes up to £100, or £200 or more. That would certainly cut down on the number of smokers, and it would do it overnight.

But think of all that lovely tax revenue that the Government would lose. £7.68 on every pack of 20 sold in the UK. They don't want to lose that. So they put the tax up a little at a time, balancing their greed (because that's what it is, it has ***nothing*** to do with improving the health of the nation) with the smokers' need to continue smoking. Then they can hold their hands up and piously state how much they're doing to curb the problems that tobacco causes. Hypocrites.

As a smoker, you are lied to over and over again. The tobacco companies with their claims of 'smooth, mellow flavour' and the image they project of the cool, sexy smoker, and the Government with their equally sleazy claims to be helping people to quit.

Absolute garbage, the lot of it. Obscene, disgusting lies from obscene, disgusting people. People who on both sides are lining their pockets with the proceeds of your illness and death. **And you're letting them do it! You're giving them that money!**

I believe that you would much rather be able to turn round to those sub-human creatures, stick up two fingers (or one, if that's your preference) and choose from any of a number of available phrases, each ending with the word 'off'.

Think long and hard about it. I encourage you to be angry – very angry. I know I am. Anger is a powerful weapon that you can use to get you through that vital first two-week period when your cravings will be at their strongest.

In the darkest hour ahead, when you want a ciggie, when you really, really want a ciggie, think of the slobbering, fat, jewellery-bedecked psychopath lying on the deck of his yacht in the brilliant sunshine. He looks up at you, holding his fat, pudgy, sweaty, diamond ring-encrusted fingers towards you.

***'Go on,'* he says, *'give me your money!'***

# Women: Conception and Pregnancy

If you are trying to conceive, or are already pregnant, then you need to look very carefully at what smoking is doing to that process.

All of the dire consequences mentioned previously affect women as well as men, but I'm afraid there's even worse news for the ladies. It is more difficult for a female body to dispose of the toxic chemicals caused by smoking than it is for a male body to. That doesn't mean it's easy for a man to rid himself of the toxins, it's anything but. It just means that it's *even harder* for a woman.

If your partner smokes, this may cause you problems if you're trying to conceive. As has been mentioned before, the toxins in cigarette smoke damage the antioxidants in the bloodstream. These antioxidants work within the semen to protect the sperm from damage. Smoking can lead to reduced sperm count and a reduction in sperm motility. In turn, this can lead to difficulty in conceiving.

Studies have also shown that smoking can actually reduce the number of eggs in the ovaries, and also lead to premature ageing of the eggs that remain. This means that if you smoke, not only is your fertility reduced but that it will remain so after you have quit.

Smoking also causes blockages in the fallopian tubes, preventing sperm and egg from meeting. This can also increase the risk of **ectopic pregnancies** – pregnancies that occur *outside* the womb. The pregnancy might occur in the cervix, in the fallopian tubes or elsewhere in the abdomen.

Along with the expected symptoms of pregnancy (missed periods, breast tenderness etc.), cramping (sometimes severe) in the lower abdomen can occur, along with vaginal bleeding. If the pregnancy occurs in a fallopian tube, this can cause the tube to rupture, tear or burst. This causes severe internal bleeding and requires ***immediate medical attention***. If this happens to you, you *must* call for an ambulance immediately.

Women who smoke are also more at risk of suffering a miscarriage. This can be caused by damaged eggs being fertilised or through damaged uterine lining.

Women are born with their full complement of eggs already fully formed, whereas men produce new sperm throughout the whole of their lives. This is why very old men can father children, whereas very old women cannot become pregnant. So by smoking, which reduces the number and viability of your eggs, you are reducing the length of your fertile life. Once they're gone, they're gone.

If you smoke during pregnancy, then you may expect certain consequences on your developing baby. As shown earlier, smoking reduces the supply of oxygen to your organs. Of course, it also reduces the amount of oxygen available to the developing foetus. The baby's organs are starved of oxygen even whilst they are developing.

One of those organs that gets starved of oxygen is the brain. Children born to smokers can have lower intelligence than non-smokers' children. They can be prone to behavioural problems and learning difficulties.

Babies born to smokers are smaller, weaker and often born prematurely. Their organs are smaller than those of babies born to non-smoking mothers. They are more prone to cot death (SIDS, or Sudden Infant Death Syndrome) and are likely to grow up weaker, more prone to illness and more likely to develop a smoking habit themselves.

Infant mortality is an alarming 50% more likely amongst babies born to smoking mothers as opposed to non-smoking mothers.

If you are trying to conceive or if you are already pregnant, then you absolutely must stop smoking straight away. There is no option. You are putting the life and future of your baby at considerable risk if you don't stop now.

## Men: Sexual Problems Can Be Cured!

Mentioned many times before is the deprivation of oxygen that smoking causes. This oxygen deprivation can lead to two serious sexual problems – erectile dysfunction and impotence. Both these conditions can be treated effectively once you have stopped smoking.

Bear in mind that problems 'getting it up' can be ***early warning signs of developing cardiovascular illnesses***. If you have issues in this area, giving up smoking is probably the very best thing that you can do to reverse the problem, and potentially prevent even worse problems further down the line.

According to *The Journal of Sexual Medicine,* it takes just three months from quitting smoking for 75% of smokers suffering from erectile dysfunction to return to full functionality. That's got to be worth giving up smokes for!

As mentioned in the previous section (if you didn't read that bit, men, I'll repeat it for you now), the toxins in cigarette smoke damage the antioxidants in the bloodstream. These antioxidants work within the semen to protect the sperm from damage. Smoking can lead to reduced sperm count and a reduction in sperm motility. In turn, this can lead to difficulty in conceiving.

# You'll Get Your Senses of Smell and Taste Back

Many smokers are actually unaware of how damaged their senses of taste and smell are. To be brutally honest, nobody with fully functioning taste buds could actually smoke a cigarette, and nobody with a fully functioning sense of smell could fail to be revolted by the smell that lingers in houses, on clothes, in hair and on skin.

People who live with smokers have their own senses dulled by the constant exposure to the numbing effects of the smoke.

It will take a short time for your senses to return to their proper working levels after you quit, but after a week or two, you'll start to notice that food is becoming tastier, that you can smell things more clearly, and the world around you is becoming a richer, more vibrant place.

Why deny yourself some of life's greatest pleasures? Imagine swilling a luscious red wine around in a glass, and smelling all the rich aromas, and being able to identify them, and then taking a sip and having the flavours explode on your tongue.

As a smoker, you are denying yourself pleasures such as these. If you are currently a smoker, then although you may not realise it, everything you can smell and taste is flat, ashy and uninteresting. The people around you who do not smoke are enjoying a far more varied sensory world than you. Why not join them? You'll be glad you did, I guarantee it.

## Final Thoughts

To round off this session, here's a list of reasons why you should quit smoking. Not all are completely serious, but we've had plenty of serious things to think about today! I've put these thoughts in the first person ('I' rather than 'you') so that you can read them to yourself and see which ones strike a chord with you.

1. I will improve my health very quickly.
2. I will improve my chances of living longer.
3. I will stop poisoning myself.
4. I will stop poisoning other people.
5. The people I love will be healthier.
6. The people I love will live longer.
7. I will stop smelling really bad.
8. My clothes will stop smelling really bad.
9. My house will stop smelling really bad.
10. I won't spend most of my life gagging for my next cigarette.

11. I won't have to leave the building and stand in the cold and rain.
12. I will look better.
13. My skin will look healthier.
14. I won't get as many wrinkles.
15. People will no longer recoil at my stale smoke breath.
16. I'll feel more confident.
17. I won't need to worry about early impotence.
18. I will have fewer problems conceiving.
19. My baby will be healthier.
20. I can stop worrying about what smoking is doing to me.
21. I can stop doing the 'smoker's dance', patting every pocket to find the lighter.
22. This book will help me stop smoking and remain forever a non-smoker.
23. My fingers won't be stained.
24. My teeth and gums won't be stained.
25. My cough will get better.
26. I'll stop wheezing.
27. I'll be able to walk further and do more physical tasks.
28. I'll be able to smell and taste properly again.
29. I'll never panic again at the thought of running out of cigarettes.
30. I'll never spend time searching for the smoking area again.
31. I won't end up with an oxygen cylinder.

32. I won't ever again have clothes with little burned holes in them.
33. I won't set fire to my house because of an insufficiently stubbed-out cigarette.
34. In a short while, my life expectancy will be the same as a non-smoker.
35. I'll find flying much more relaxing.
36. I can take longer flights – maybe go somewhere more interesting.
37. I can have a great holiday every year with the saved money.
38. I could put down the deposit on – or buy – a nice new car.
39. I will live to see my children grow up.
40. I will live to see my grandchildren.
41. I won't feel like an outcast any more.
42. I won't need to worry about my lungs looking like a pair of kippers.
43. My partner will be more willing to kiss me.
44. I'll make new friends, who may previously have been put off by the smoke.
45. I'll be a good role model for my kids.
46. My kids will be less likely to become smokers themselves.
47. I will be less stressed.
48. Tobacco company executives can kiss my ****.
49. The Treasury can kiss my ****.
50. I will be free.

All this can be yours. You have the keys to success in your hand.

Now you should spend a little time thinking about your own reasons to quit. You **do** need to have a reason – a good reason. Any or all of the reasons mentioned in this session will do. Don't pick one because I say you have to have one, though. You must find a reason and ***truly make it your own***. Hold it (or them) in your heart, and always be ready to remind yourself of just why you're giving up.

It can be very helpful to have a little visual reminder about your person of why exactly it is that you have quit. A small photograph of a loved one, for example. You could write on the back 'I've given up for you'.

Why not make the wallpaper or screensaver on your mobile phone, tablet or computer a picture of the loved one you are doing this for? You can look at it any time you want, and nobody else needs know what it means to you.

Or you could have a picture of a shiny new car that you'd like, or a sunny, palm-lined beach. Your reasons are your own. Keep them at the front of your mind.

Take a break now. Don't read the next session until tomorrow. Let the thoughts in this session sink in and take root.

See you tomorrow for the next session: Preparing to Quit.

PS – Don't forget to read the Introduction to the Hypnotherapy Recording next. You can do that right now.

# Introduction to the Hypnotherapy Recordings

At this point, you should begin listening to the 30-minute hypnotherapy session that comes free with this book. If you have already listened to it, that's OK, but from now on you should listen to it **once per day.**

If you haven't already done so, you should now download the recordings from quitsmokebook.com/hypnosessions. The recording is in mp3 format.

For the best results, you should transfer the recording to a music player like an iPod, or onto your phone or tablet.

You should listen through headphones.

You will need to find yourself somewhere quiet and peaceful to go to in order to listen to the session. It's very important that you are not disturbed for about half an hour. You need to make this clear to anyone else in the house.

The second recording is a shorter version of the 30-minute session, and you should only listen to this when you ***absolutely can't*** manage 30 minutes.

**Try not to listen to the shorter version regularly.**

Only use this when you really, really can't spare 30 minutes. This shorter session lasts just 15 minutes and as such is not as effective as the full session.

Giving up smoking is ***important.*** You can afford a paltry half an hour – it will be massively beneficial to you.

Having said that (and I really do mean it), I have also provided two other recordings. One lasts five minutes and the final one a mere two minutes.

Use the five-minute recording at any time, whenever you need it. It will serve to reinforce the message and can be used at any time of day, but again – **not when you're driving or doing anything that requires your attention.**

The two-minute recording is like an emergency booster. When you feel the craving is getting too much for you, just sit back, close your eyes and listen for two minutes. If you feel self-conscious doing this in public, find a private spot where nobody will disturb you for a couple of minutes. You could even go to the toilet if there's nowhere more salubrious that you can use!

Use these two shorter recordings at any time, as often as you feel the need. They will help to fortify you against the worst.

Do try to listen to the longer recordings as often as you can. These contain much more force, especially the 30-minute recording. I know it's a pain to take half an hour out of your busy day, but you do want to succeed, don't you?

You can listen to the recording either sitting down in a comfortable chair or lying on a couch or bed. If you are sitting on a chair, get comfortable first, place your hands in your lap and your feet flat on the floor. Take off your shoes.

**Do not listen to this recording if you are driving or operating any kind of machinery. Do not listen to this recording whilst doing something else. Listening to the recording should be done away from any distractions.**

Once you are settled and comfortable, you can begin listening. You will be guided into a light, trance-like state. The trance is very light and if you do need to deal with some emergency, you'll find that you can do so with no difficulty.

This is not stage hypnotism which relies on tricks and showmanship to make people do things they would not normally do. It's more like drifting into a daydream. No suggestions are made that are not beneficial to you.

You may find that you start drifting off during the hypnotherapy session, and you can't remember the words. That's alright.

The words are aimed at your subconscious, and that remains alert even when you aren't paying attention.

The recording uses techniques from neuro-linguistic programming (NLP) which has proved very beneficial in the treatment of smokers who wish to quit.

Although some people report that a single session with a hypnotherapist has made them quit smoking forever, it is the repetition that drives it home for most people. With this in mind, you should listen to the therapy session every day, preferably at about the same time each day, if you can manage it.

Before you embark on the hypnotherapy sessions, I want to teach you a breathing technique.

What? Don't we all know how to breathe?

Well, yes and no. Many of us have 'bad breathing habits', and being a smoker really doesn't help. Here's a way to improve your breathing technique, relax and help to overcome those cravings.

Firstly, sit yourself down in a comfortable chair. Eventually, you'll be able to do this anywhere, but for now, make yourself comfortable. Don't cross your legs, but place your feet flat on the floor. If it's possible, take off your shoes. Cup your hands and place them palm upwards in your lap, or rest your arms on the arms of the chair.

Now close your eyes.

Sit still for a while and gently bring your attention to your breathing. Is your chest expanding as you breathe in or is it your tummy? If your chest is expanding as you breathe, then you've developed bad breathing habits. Switch your breathing so that your tummy expands and not your chest. Like a baby. This is called diaphragmatic breathing, and is the most efficient breathing method.

Breathe in through your nose and out through your mouth. Take a long, deep breath in through your nose. Hold it for a slow count of three then let it out through your mouth. As you exhale, let your shoulders drop and relax.

Breathe in again, slowly and deeply, through your nose. Hold the breath for a slow count of three, then let it go through your mouth, again allowing your shoulders to drop and relax even more.

Again.

Now return to your normal breathing pattern (but remembering to breathe diaphragmatically).

Feel your stresses fall away through your feet and into the ground.

This whole process should take about 30 seconds. You can do it any time, anywhere. Just not when you're driving, OK?

With practice, you'll find this a very effective method of de-stressing, and if you do it regularly, it will help considerably in the days ahead.

# 3

# Session 3: Preparing to Quit

Right. This is where the real work starts. We've talked about why we smoke, and all the horrible things that smoking does to our health and the health of people around us. Now it's time, at last, to **do something about it**.

Before we get stuck in, I really want to congratulate you on getting this far. I know we haven't actually taken the plunge yet, but you've read through all the horrible stuff – I'm sure you must feel that you've been lectured, even scolded, often enough by people telling you what harm you're doing, but **that stops now**.

You've accepted that smoking is bad and that you need to give up. You've thought long and hard about your personal reasons for quitting, and you're holding tightly on to them. Seriously, ***well done***.

Now is the time to prepare yourself for the quitting process. I'm sure you know this all too well – you may have tried quitting before, maybe many times – but I'm going to tell you anyway – *this won't be easy*. In fact, it will probably be very difficult. Don't be despondent though. You **can** do it. You really can. Together, we'll get you through this and in no time, you'll achieve your desire of being smoke-free.

Preparation is a key aspect of a successful quitting strategy. I found this simple mnemonic from the American National Cancer Institute. It puts what you have to do simply and clearly:

**S – Set** a date on which you will quit.

**T – Tell** your family, friends and workmates that you plan to quit.

**A – Anticipate** and plan for the difficulties you'll face whilst quitting.

**R – Remove** all tobacco products from your home, car, place of work and anywhere else you go regularly.

**T – Talk** to a doctor about getting help to quit.

That's the strategy we're going to follow, and we'll be looking in more detail at each of the five stages in this session.

Before we dive into the S-T-A-R-T strategy, let's have a quick look at the options for quitting that are available to you at this point.

## Cutting Down

This is a method tried by many would-be quitters. The idea is that you could slowly reduce the number of cigarettes you smoke in a day until ultimately you end up not smoking at all.

Say you smoke ten cigarettes a day. You'd start by smoking just nine for a day or two. Then you'd just smoke eight for a couple of days after that. Then after two or three weeks, you'd naturally arrive at the magic zero cigarettes per day, and that would be that. Job done.

Sounds reasonable, doesn't it? Unfortunately, this technique totally fails to take into account the effect that the nicotine addiction has on your body, and, to be brutally honest, your ability to think straight whilst under the influence of that addiction.

For example, let's say that you're at the stage when you cut down to five cigarettes a day. You've had your five, then you get a difficult telephone call. To ease the stress it's caused you, you light up a cigarette. Well, it's only six instead of five, isn't it?

By allowing yourself to backslide, you will have undone all the good work you've done to get to the five-a-day stage. ***You have given yourself permission to fail***. No doubt, a flood of relief will follow. Actually, it's alright to have a smoke when you're stressed. Phew! You don't have to give up smoking at all!

Then you're straight back to stage one. You'll continue smoking for another few months or years, then the old thoughts will come back, and you'll try to give up yet again.

**The secret is not to *try* to give up… Just. Give. Up.**

There are any number of psychological and physiological reasons why it is more likely that you will fail to quit if you take what seems like the easy route of cutting down. The simple fact that you need to bear in mind is that you are ***90% more likely to fail*** to quit if you try to do it by cutting down. It's **not** an easy route to success. ***It's an almost certain route to failure***.

**Takeaway: Cutting down is the one method tried by most would-be quitters. It is the one method that you *must* avoid.**

# Nicotine Patches / Nicotine Gum

As we have explored in previous sessions, the really dangerous chemicals in cigarettes come from tar. These are mostly not in themselves addictive, it is the nicotine that causes the habit.

The cravings that you experience for a smoke is a craving for nicotine, not for the toxic soup of chemicals that come with it in tobacco.

One answer is to find a substitute form of nicotine which does not have all that nasty baggage with it. This is where nicotine patches and gum can be useful.

The nicotine patch attaches to your skin, like a sticking plaster, and then allows a measured quantity of nicotine to seep into your bloodstream over a period of several hours. This has been shown to work well, particularly with heavy smokers, whose dependence on nicotine may be severe.

If you do opt for patches, you should heed one very important warning. The patch passes a measured quantity of nicotine into your bloodstream, which means that you have a 'safe' amount of the drug in your system. If you smoke whilst wearing a patch, you can easily overdose on the drug, leading to nicotine poisoning.

If you are wearing a patch, **you must not smoke**.

Nicotine gum does a similar thing, but with the gum, you have to regulate your intake yourself.

If you are thinking of using either patches or gum, ***it is very strongly advised that you consult with your doctor first***. They will be able to give you all the advice you need about the use and abuse of these replacement therapies.

Before you decide, though, there's one very important fact to consider. Whilst switching from cigarettes to a less harmful alternative can be seen as a huge step forward, you must remember that whilst you might now be rid of the toxic miasma of cigarette smoke, *you will still be addicted to nicotine.*

You will still at some point, have to wean yourself off that highly addictive drug. Only some of the good things that happen when you stop smoking (as listed in Session 2) will actually happen. The excess stress that smokers put themselves under will still be with you, because it is the nicotine addiction that causes the stress, not the other stuff.

Your body will continue to crave nicotine, and it knows full well that it can relieve that craving, if only temporarily, by having a cigarette.

## e-Cigarettes / Vaping

This is currently a very popular method of quitting smoking. An electronic cigarette (e-cigarette or e-cig) is a device of similar proportions to a cigarette. Sometimes it is made to look very much like a real cigarette, sometimes it is quite different in appearance.

It consists of three basic parts:

1. A cartridge containing liquid nicotine (and maybe some other stuff – see below)

2. A vaporising chamber

3. A rechargeable battery

The user purchases a nicotine cartridge, which often has flavourings added, and fits it into the device. The liquid nicotine is heated and atomised in the vaporisation chamber and the resulting vapour is inhaled by the user.

The theory is that nicotine is being supplied to the addict without all the noxious chemicals associated with tobacco smoke. No burning takes place at all, it is purely vapour that the user inhales, not smoke.

Although it cannot be doubted that e-cigarettes are **safer** than tobacco cigarettes, questions remain over whether they are **actually SAFE** or not.

Firstly, there is the ever-present issue of drug addiction. Use of e-cigarettes does not address the addict's dependency on the drug at all. It simply provides another method for the addict to get their 'fix'. Make no bones about it, if you swap your tobacco habit for a vaping habit, you are still a nicotine addict, and all the provisos that go with nicotine patches and nicotine gum apply here as well. You will not overcome your cravings, and the stress factors introduced by your addiction will not go away.

Secondly, there is the issue of what is actually in the nicotine cartridges. In 2009 the US Food and Drug Administration conducted a study of nicotine cartridges. They found that the amount of delivered nicotine stated on the label did not match the actual amount delivered. Some cartridges marked as nicotine-free were found to contain nicotine.

Even more alarmingly, some cartridges were found to contain toxic chemicals, such as ethylene glycol, the principal component in anti-freeze.

Studies have also indicated that taking up vaping may not be the ultimate solution to smoking that some manufacturers have claimed it to be. It has been found that a large proportion of vapers also smoke tobacco cigarettes. The use of e-cigs, it seems, may not cut out smoking altogether.

The World Health Organisation has said that it remains to be demonstrated that vaping is safe and that the vapour inhaled by the user may not be as danger-free as some manufacturers would have us believe.

Sadly, there may also be dangers associated with second-hand vapour (called 'passive vaping'), so the health of people around the user may also be at risk.

Thirdly, there is the cost. Whilst not as high as that of smoking tobacco cigarettes, it is still considerable. A cartridge of liquid nicotine for use in an e-cigarette typically lasts as long as a pack of 20 cigarettes (longer if the user is economical with their inhalations), and a regular user of e-cigarettes can still rack up a bill of hundreds of pounds in a year.

A fourth consideration that has caused some alarm recently is the appeal vaping may have to children. The sale of vaping kits is not regulated in the way that the sale of tobacco products is. Vaping kits and refills can be bought very easily online, and there are very few sellers who will effectively check the age of their customers. Just before writing these words, I went online to look at vaping products. Only two of the websites I visited had any age-verification checks at all. In both cases it was a simple choice – click 'I am under 18' or 'I am over 18'. That's not going to stop kids, is it?

If you're still thinking of taking up vaping, you may want to consider this: On 17th May 2018, BBC News reported that TV producer Tallmadge Wakeman ('Wake') D'Elia, 35, died when his vape exploded, sending fragments into his skull. His house also caught fire as a result of the explosion. Firefighters called to the scene discovered his body.

Between 2009 and 2016 there were 195 reported incidents of e-cigarettes exploding, many causing fires, in the US alone. As a result, there were 133 injuries requiring treatment, 38 of which were classed as 'severe'.

One of these incidents involved a 29-year old man from Colorado, whose e-cigarette exploded in his face, shattering his teeth and breaking his neck.

Whilst it cannot be denied that switching from tobacco (combustible) cigarettes to e-cigarettes is a step in the right direction, it should still be treated with caution as an option. Consider the following:

**Seven reasons why vaping may not be the answer:**

1. You will still be addicted to nicotine.

2. Your stress levels will not improve.

3. What you and the people around you are inhaling may not be safe.

4. It may not stop you smoking.

5. It will still be costing you to keep up your habit.

6. You may unwittingly be encouraging children to vape, or even smoke.

7. Your vape pen may explode and injure or even kill you.

The conclusion to be drawn from this is that no matter how appealing vaping may seem, it is not as safe as the proven Nicotine Replacement Therapies such as nicotine patches and nicotine gum.

The bottom line is that there is **NOTHING** as good for you as *simply giving up.*

OK, we've looked at some of the alternatives. Let's now look in more detail at the **S.T.A.R.T.** method.

# 1. Set a Date

The first decision you must make is the date on which you will stop smoking forever. It sounds easy enough, but it's an important psychological step. Don't make the date too soon, and don't place it in the too distant future. A week from now is about right, though you can stretch it a little further away if you really feel you need to.

This is the day on which you let go of your dependency. It is the day when you take your first steps into freedom. It is the day when **everything** starts to get better.

On your Quit Day you will smoke one cigarette, and no more. It will be the last one you ever smoke.

You should look forward to this day on the days leading up to it. See it as your portal to a new, healthier and wealthier life. Every day leading up to this day is important. You should examine your feelings every time you light up a cigarette.

- Why am I smoking this thing?

- Do I really NEED it?

- What is it doing to my body?

- How does it make me smell?

- How much is it costing me?

- Could I just stub it out and go back inside instead?

- How much better will I feel when I don't have to come out here?

- How much better will I feel when I know I am not killing myself?

- What shall I do with all that money I'm saving? (Really go to town on this one).

As your Quit Day approaches, talk with people you know who have given up. Ask them how they feel, how they got over the cravings. Encourage them to tell you how much better they feel. Friends who have already quit will be a real support network as you beat your own cravings.

I strongly recommend that you set your Quit Day on a normal rest day. For most people, Saturday would be best, but adjust this to suit your own schedule. If you quit on a working day, there could be too many trigger situations for you to deal effectively with.

You should plan to do something special and a bit different on your chosen Quit Day. Get out of the house – brooding at home will make the day more difficult.

Take a trip to the country or to the beach – somewhere where you can get loads of fresh air.

Alternatively, plan a trip to an art gallery, a museum, a theatre or a cinema if that takes your fancy. Go bowling, perhaps. These are all places that can take your mind off your immediate cravings – and smoking is banned in them, so you won't be troubled by other people smoking near you.

## 2. Tell Everyone that You're Quitting

It's very important that your friends, family and loved ones know that you are going to quit. They should encourage you to do so. If one of your friends tries to dissuade you, or constantly insists on telling you how difficult it will be, then you need to re-examine the basis of your friendship. You need to ask yourself – and them – ***why*** they want you to continue this extremely harmful practice. That is not a desire that a true friend would have.

Reject negative advice and bear in mind the above.

You will probably find that your friends and family (especially the non-smokers among them) will be delighted at the news. It's very hard to watch a loved one slowly killing themselves, and knowing that you're going to stop doing it should fill them with joy.

One of the very best ways to ensure success at quitting is to quit with somebody else. There must be some amongst your smoking friends and/or family who also want to quit. Talk it over with them. Discuss what you've read so far in this book, and make a pact.

You can support each other through the worst of the cravings. In helping another, you will be helping yourself. If your quit-friend phones you up to admit to strong cravings, you can talk them out of it. You will have to be the strong one, and in acting like the strong one, you will **become truly strong!**

By telling everyone that you're quitting, you will be setting up an expectation amongst them that you will succeed. It will be much harder for you to crumple at the first hurdle and light up a crafty one. You will not only be letting yourself down, you'll be letting them down, too.

The knowledge that other people have an expectation of you will make you more likely to succeed – considerably so. No one wants to see that look of disappointment in a friend or loved-one's face when you admit to failure, or even worse, if they catch you smoking after you've promised to stop.

Ask your friends and family to be supportive. Ask them to encourage you in the struggle ahead. It will be a struggle, but really not for very long – just a couple of weeks, usually – and the constant support and encouragement will help more than you can imagine.

It's also important to let your workmates know that you will be quitting. Don't be afraid to ask for their support – most people will gladly help someone who is working to overcome an addiction. You may discover many allies, and some unexpected sources of help and encouragement among your colleagues.

# 3. Anticipate the Problems Ahead

There's no denying that there will be problems ahead. You are an addict, and you will suffer from withdrawal symptoms. I won't pretend that this will be easy. If it was easy, you wouldn't need this book to get you through it. Some of the symptoms you may experience are as follows:

**Craving**. This is the addiction at work. Your body has developed a dependency on nicotine and now it's being denied its regular fix.

**Restlessness**. You may feel twitchy and unable to relax.

**Tiredness**. Your inability to relax and a constant tension will inevitably lead to poor sleep and subsequent tiredness.

**Poor concentration**. A combination of tiredness and distraction by the craving can lead to poor levels of concentration.

**Irritability**. All the above will almost certainly make you tetchy and irritable. You may find that you snap at people more easily than you would before you gave up.

**Frustration**. Your lack of sleep and poorer than average concentration will mean that you can't do things as well as you should be able to. You will probably feel frustrated, and quite probably angry. Your anger will mostly be directed at yourself, but you may also be lashing out at people around you, who don't really deserve it.

The tiredness, lack of concentration, irritability and frustration will have a knock-on effect on people around you. One of the main purposes of telling everyone around you that you are quitting smoking is to prepare them for exactly these things. If they are aware that your body is fighting an addiction, they will understand your change of mood better, and give you more room. You will almost certainly recognise when you are being angry or irritable. A little part of your mind that is somehow disconnected from the rest, the part that always remains calm and sober, will let you know. Once you've calmed yourself – and we'll look at ways of doing this in a minute – just say 'Sorry' to the person you've lashed out at. They'll understand.

You may find after a few days that you begin to suffer from what quitters often call 'brain-fog'. It's an inability to think as clearly as you would normally. You may become easily confused or puzzled by what would normally be straightforward situations. It can be quite disconcerting, even a little frightening.

**Don't worry!** This is a common symptom. You are gaining the upper hand over your addiction, and your body will now throw everything it has at you in an attempt to get you back on the nicotine. Stay strong – it won't last and you **will** win!

**Physical symptoms**. Sometimes, the withdrawal can manifest itself in physical conditions such as tired and aching limbs and headaches. Some quitters even record that they felt woozy or dizzy. This can be quite alarming, but be aware that it usually only lasts for one or two days.

**Depression**. Your body is desperately trying to get you to suck in some nicotine, and it's doing everything it can to force you to do this. You may well feel depressed, with great worry for the future. It will pass, and more quickly than you think. It's a big mistake to think that the rest of your life will be as bad as the first couple of weeks. **It won't**. The cravings grow weaker and weaker until they are gone completely. Remember that no matter how bad you feel right now, this is temporary, and will be over before you know it.

**Hunger**. We touched on this in a previous session. Some newly ex-smokers attempt to satisfy their nicotine cravings by eating more. This doesn't really work, and just falls into the category of 'comfort-eating', which we all do occasionally. Be aware of it and be prepared. Have a pack of sugar-free mints or similar to hand.

You may be alarmed at how quickly these effects of withdrawal begin to manifest themselves. They may begin within an hour or two of you stubbing out your final cigarette. I've mentioned this more than once, but it's worth mentioning again; these withdrawal symptoms typically last for ***no more than two weeks***. It is often reported that the symptoms and the cravings reach a peak at around day ten or eleven. Odd as this may sound, when it gets really bad, it means that you're on the cusp of beating it. It's like a last-ditch effort to force you back to smoking. Once you break through that, the addiction has nothing left to throw at you.

When you notice one of these symptoms, the best thing to do is to acknowledge it, remember that you have anticipated it, and move on. Don't give it any power over you. You are in charge. Remember all the time. '***This won't last. Just a few more days.***'

Anticipation of the effects of withdrawal is vital. It's half the battle. Remember the old adage: ***Forewarned is forearmed.*** It means you are prepared for them, and have drawn up ways of dealing with them.

This is what we're going to look at now.

You need to bear in mind that not only is there a drug withdrawal to beat, there are also certain habits that go with that addiction. Certain behaviours and actions that your body is used to performing, which you will now have to forget. For example, a lot of quitters say that they don't know what to do with their hands. This is because they are used to the action of lighting up, holding a cigarette and constantly moving it up to their mouth and back down again.

If you have tried to quit in the past and have failed, think back to that time and try to remember what techniques you used, if any, to help you succeed. Maybe some of these things that you did were actually helping. Something else may have dragged you back down to being a smoker. Alternatively, there may well be things that you can be certain didn't help.

Sort out in your mind what seemed to be working and what definitely wasn't. That will give you a basic list of dos and don'ts.

It doesn't matter if you don't have a list, or if your list looks small and insignificant. Here are a few more techniques that can help you get past the cravings:

1. Find an inert substitute that you can put in your mouth. Part of the habit of smoking is having something in your mouth. In the past, some people advocated using an unlit cigarette. **Don't!** You can see where that will end up. I had a close friend once, who was giving up smoking. I didn't see him at work, only in the evenings, when he sat around with an unlit cigarette drooping from his mouth. Without fail, he would say something like 'I'm just popping out for a breath of fresh air.' When he came back the cigarette was gone. When asked where it had gone, he said 'Oh, I don't need it. I threw it away.' Our noses told us how he had disposed of it! Use something harmless, like a cocktail stick or a pencil.

2. Drink plenty of water. Have a glass of water by you all the time. When the urge for a cigarette comes, take a few small sips. Roll the water round in your mouth and think about what it is doing. Water is essential for all of us, it is literally a life-giver. One of the effects of smoking is dehydration. By drinking plenty water, you are starting straight away to reverse the effects that the smoke has had on you. It is cleaning you on the inside.

3. When the urge to smoke comes, stand up and take a short walk. No more than five minutes. If you are in a situation where it is possible, do a little light exercise, a few star jumps, anything to increase your heart rate a little and get that blood pumping. An alternative would be to walk up and down the stairs two or three times, if stairs are available.

4. At least to start with, avoid situations which you associate with smoking – remember again ***this will normally only be for a couple of weeks***, until you are strong enough to face those situations confidently. If your usual smoking friends invite you to come outside with them on their smoking breaks, you ***absolutely must not go!*** Your friends are most likely only being kind, and they may be missing your company, but the temptation will be extremely strong to join them in a quick smoke. I had a colleague at work who gave up smoking, but continued to go out for breaks with his smoking friends. Within days, he was smoking again. Be polite, **but just say 'No, thank you.'**

5. Take up a new pastime that will not be associated with smoking.

6. Find yourself a big, clear glass or plastic jar. Place it somewhere prominent in your house where you will see it every day. Once you have quit, every day put the money you would have spent on cigarettes into the jar. Watch that money grow and keep thinking what you're going to do with it. Make plans. Talk about them.

7. Be proud of yourself. When you get the urge, feel a little swell of self-admiration for caring enough about yourself and those around you to become an ex-smoker.

8. Prepare a list of the reasons why you are quitting smoking. Take your time over it. Use nice paper and a good pen. Write it carefully and with thought. Fold it neatly and carry it around with you everywhere or take a picture of it with your phone or tablet. Whenever you feel the urge to smoke, pull it out and read slowly and carefully through it. If it's on your phone or tablet, you might want to make it your wallpaper.

9. If you are ever offered a cigarette, say 'I don't smoke, thank you.' **Don't** say 'I'm trying to give them up.' That's

feeble. You are not **trying** to give them up. **You <u>have</u> given them up and you are an <u>ex-smoker</u>.**

## 4. Remove All Cigarettes and Associated Items from Your Environment.

The day before your set quit day, go around the house, the car, the office – anywhere where you are likely to spend time over the next month or so – and carefully and thoroughly remove anything associated with smoking. Cigarettes, matches, lighters, ashtrays, the lot.

Physically remove the ashtray and the cigarette lighter from the car. Ask someone to keep them for you and to return them **only** if you're selling the car.

Seeing smoking paraphernalia around you all the time will discourage you from your goal of giving up. If they're not there, they can't taunt you, so get rid. If you like, put everything into a box and give it to a non-smoking friend. Ask them

never to give it back to you, under any circumstances, but not to get rid of it just yet. In a few weeks, you'll be strong enough to tell your friend to dispose of it.

This action will prevent you from bin-diving in desperation during your time of craving. Unlikely, I know, but it could happen!

Retain one cigarette and one match. This will be your last cigarette and you will smoke it on your Quit Day.

## 5. Talk to Your Doctor About Quitting

These days there is a huge amount of support to help you to quit smoking. Your first port of call should be your doctor. He or she has detailed information about your personal health and will be able to advise you in a very personal way that identifies your individual needs. If you need to, you should make regular appointments with your doctor to keep them up to date with your progress. You can also discuss any concerns that you have, and any problems you may have encountered.

If you are on medication, your prescription may have to be reviewed to take into account the effects of your quitting. Only your doctor can do this for you.

The NHS provides some great advice and support for quitters, which can be found here:

www.nhs.uk/livewell/smoking

Support groups are available all over the place. If you would like to join a group, you'll be made very welcome.

To find local support near you, start here:

www.nhs.uk/smokefree/help-and-advice/local-support-services-helplines

Above all, believe in yourself. You know you need to do this. You know that you can do this. You know that you are now an ex-smoker.

Big day tomorrow... see you there.

# 4

## Session 4: Quitting

Well, here we are. The big day.

This is the day that you *take control of your health, wealth and your life*.

I strongly recommend that you quit on a rest day. For most people working a five-day week, this would be Saturday. This gives you two days without the stresses of the work environment.

Before you smoke your last cigarette, check that all the following has been done:

- You have anticipated the problems and difficulties that you will probably face, as listed in the previous session.
- You have thought about strategies to combat them.
- You have talked to your friends, relatives and work colleagues, and told them that you will be quitting smoking.
- You have their support and encouragement.
- You have removed all smoking paraphernalia from your house, car, office and anywhere else you are likely to be in the next few weeks.
- You have spoken with your doctor about the best strategies for you personally.

When you can answer 'yes' to all the above, then you're ready.

You're probably feeling quite anxious at the moment. That's OK. That's fine. It's perfectly natural. It would be foolish to think that quitting will be easy. Those who do think that will probably fail. You won't.

You are prepared for the difficulties ahead, and you've got ways to deal with them.

As you smoke your last cigarette now, I want you to think about all the damage that it's doing to your body. Think about the damage it's doing to your friends and family. Think about the pain and grief that lies ahead for you and your loved ones if you fail to quit now. Think about that greedy tobacco company board member who just wants you to give them all your money then go away and die. Think about the anonymous, dreary taxman with the dead eyes, who wants pretty much the same.

Now as you stub out that cigarette, see a bright future for yourself and your loved ones. See them all living long and healthy lives. See the happiness and joy in your future. See that greedy tobacco company board member sitting destitute in a gutter. See the taxman foiled. See yourself on a wonderful holiday, soaking up the sun on a palm-tree-lined tropical beach. See yourself buying that car you've always wanted. See yourself free of the beast.

That's what quitting is all about.

***Just two weeks*** and you'll virtually be there...

If there are any cigarettes left in your final pack, hand the pack to a trusted friend or loved one and tell them not to give them back to you under any circumstances. Then in a few weeks, you can tell them to throw the unwanted carton away.

## The First 24 Hours

This is your first major hurdle. The first 24 hours are likely to be the worst. Nicotine addiction is severe, but it also wears off relatively quickly as your body adjusts and begins to regain its balance.

The best advice given by huge numbers of ex-smokers is to take each moment as it arrives.

Can you give up smoking for 24 hours? It doesn't matter.

Can you give up smoking for one hour? Even that doesn't matter.

Can you give up smoking for five minutes? Of course you can. You have done many times before. You reach for a cigarette and the phone rings, so you 'give up' for the duration of the phone call. Take each minute as it comes, during the worst of the cravings.

Your body will scream out at you to have a cigarette and it will use all the weapons it has – it will be like a severe hunger. Headache, nausea, dizziness, restlessness, lack of concentration – all these things will be lined up against you.

But it's not real. Your body is trying to trick you into lighting up again. You know better, though. You know that you are strong, and that you are now a non-smoker.

You will beat the craving. It won't last forever. It won't last anything like that. Generally, just a couple of weeks and the worst will be behind you and you will have won.

Surrender like a weakling to those sneaky tricks, and you will have failed. You will be a failure.

You're not a failure, *you're a winner*. You can take each minute, each five minutes, each hour as it comes, and give up smoking for that long.

You should be aware of your smoking habits, the times when you have always had a cigarette in the past. Make a list of them so they won't sneak up on you and surprise you.

When you wake up.

Breakfast.

With a cup of coffee.

In the car on the way to work.

Waiting for the bus or train to work.

Coffee breaks at work.

Lunch.

When you're on the telephone.

More coffee breaks at work.

Driving home from work.

Waiting for the bus or train home.

When you get home.

With your evening meal.

Watching television.

Using your computer at home.

Just before you go to bed.

All these are common times for smokers to light up. You will have your own habits, your own rituals. If you're aware of them, you can prepare for them, and they will lose much of their power over you.

Follow the suggestions here, and any that you have discussed with successful quitters amongst your friends, and tough it out for 24 hours.

Once the first 24 hours is over (set an alarm clock or a reminder on your phone), you will have overcome the most difficult part. You can be pleased with yourself – you deserve to be pleased with yourself.

## Dealing With It

As soon as you've had your last cigarette, I want you to get out of the house and go for a walk. It doesn't have to be very far, just get some fresh air and a little exercise.

An excellent way of beating cravings is through diaphragmatic breathing. Refer back to the instructions on breathing technique in the Introduction to the Hypnotherapy Recordings (page 63).

Exercise will also help greatly. Get out for a walk, breathe some fresh air, stretch those legs! If it's raining, don't be put off! Enjoy the freshness that a little rain brings. If it's raining hard, use an umbrella or wear waterproofs, it's great! Enjoy being outside like you did when you were a child.

Any exercise will help, but brisk exercise is best. Once you find yourself breathing a little harder than normal, maybe feeling a little warmer than usual, then you're working at about the right level.

The deeper breathing and faster heartbeat will help to oxygenate your blood. Remember that haemoglobin clogged with carbon monoxide – clear out the toxins and replace them with good, life-sustaining oxygen!

## What to Expect to Start With

Depending on your past smoking habits, you may begin to feel symptoms of withdrawal within one or two hours. The first symptoms may be quite alarming. If you're going to get the dizziness mentioned in the last session, then this is when it is most likely to happen.

Don't be too worried about it unless it goes on for more than two days. If it does (and it's very unlikely to) you should go to see your doctor. It may be that you need some form of Nicotine Replacement Therapy, at least to start with.

Many of these early symptoms may result from other factors. You may become dehydrated. Remember to drink plenty of water. Drink at least six full glasses of water per day. Every time you feel the craving, have a drink of water. Sip, don't gulp.

Water is almost magical. For some people, a glass of water can stop nicotine cravings dead in their tracks.

For the first few days, try to avoid caffeinated drinks. Coffee can particularly be a trigger for cravings, as for a lot of smokers, a coffee and a ciggie go together.

Also, too much caffeine produces very similar effects to nicotine withdrawal, emphasising your symptoms and making it a lot harder for you.

There seem to be two schools of thought about your first days as a non-smoker. One stresses the importance of keeping to your normal schedule and normal activities, whilst the other suggests changing things for a while, to avoid the regular smoke-triggers.

I suppose which course you follow is up to you. One method may work for one person and the other for another. What I would suggest is that you don't deviate dramatically from your normal routine, but if a situation is giving you smoke-triggers that you can't handle, just back away from that situation and do something else instead. Only you will know when this happens, and you will have to make that choice when it appears. Sometimes, the strongest thing you can do is walk away.

It's important that you keep busy, both physically and mentally. Physical work will help to distract your mind. Maybe do some gardening, go for a long walk, visit the swimming baths or play with the kids outside.

If you followed the advice given in Session 3, you will have planned a great day out for yourself and/or your family or friends. Be excited about your trip, and enjoy it to the full. In the evening, perhaps you could go out for a nice meal in a good restaurant.

If you haven't planned anything, maybe do something off the cuff. Surprise yourself! Even if you really don't want to go out, you could do something at home. Work on the car, tidy the box room, have a good old clear-out.

Do *something* – something that will distract you for a few hours.

## How Should You Feel?

Being in the right frame of mind is to win half the battle. You should be immensely proud of what you are achieving. Be proud to be a non-smoker. Be defiant towards the symptoms that your body will throw at you.

You are bull-headed and you will **not** be defeated. This is your life, and **you will succeed!**

Try not to obsess about how much you want a cigarette. Remind yourself constantly of why you have given up and for whom. Ask yourself if you are prepared to go back to the terrible risks to yourself and to those around you. Are you prepared to look and smell awful again? Are you prepared to disappoint all those who are supporting you? More importantly, are you prepared to disappoint yourself?

No. No. No.

When the craving grows, try to imagine yourself physically suppressing it. Repeat to yourself – 'No, no, **no, NO!'**

See the craving as a physical being, a filthy, disgusting, depraved creature trying to drag you into its foul den, where it will kill you. See yourself forcing it back. Batter it with whatever you want.

'I am in control, not you! Get away!'

Every minute you defeat it, every hour, every day, it will get weaker and weaker, and you will get stronger and stronger, until the day that it is so feeble and pathetic that you can simply ignore it.

**Always keep in mind that these cravings WILL go away.** One day, much sooner than you imagine, you'll look back on the first few days of your becoming a non-smoker and wonder what all the fuss was about.

When the craving is at its worst and you're at your lowest level, remember that you don't need to fear the future. You don't need to be afraid that this will be your life from now on, constantly desperate for a smoke. Every minute of every hour of every day will get better and better.

If you get to the point where the craving is beginning to affect your day, if you are starting to think more and more about your desire to smoke, listen to the two-minute recording. If you're self-conscious about this, go somewhere private for a couple of minutes. If all else fails, you can always nip into the loo! Plug your earpieces in and close your eyes, literally just for two minutes, and listen to this short session. It will help.

## Cash

We have previously worked out how much you spend on cigarettes (Session 2: Reasons to Quit). We have also discussed putting this money in a clear glass jar so that you can see how much money you are saving (Session 3: Preparing to Quit).

Now is the time to begin putting your cash in that glass jar. This has a number of useful effects. Firstly, part of the ritual of smoking (giving money to someone else) is maintained by you physically removing the money from your pocket and 'handing it over' to the glass jar.

Secondly, you can see that this money has not really gone. It's there as a physical reminder of what you are saving and achieving.

However, at the beginning, I want you to use this money to reward yourself. All the saving up for Caribbean holidays can come later. For now, give yourself little treats from the jar – never more than is in there, though.

Buy a book, a CD, a DVD or a video game or a nice little piece of costume jewellery. Anything you want. A nice decoration for the house – maybe a small statue to stand on your mantelpiece, or a picture to hang on the wall – can be there constantly to remind you of why you gave up and what you've achieved. When you have bought your little gift to yourself, hold it in your hands and have a good look at it. Tell yourself that if you hadn't given up smoking, you would not have this item.

The money you save from not buying tobacco will build up quickly and the expensive treats and rewards can come later, but for now, just treasure your new purchase and see it as the first of many, many fine things that are coming your way.

# Recording Your Feelings

Some people find it very helpful to keep a record of their feelings and triumphs during the initial quitting period. Buy yourself a nice notebook and have it to hand at all times. When you feel the craving begin to appear, start writing down how you feel.

Likewise, when you overcome this feeling, write down how you overcame it and how you feel about your success.

When the craving comes again – slightly less intensely next time – it can be helpful to read back over your previous experiences. You should notice that your feelings this time are slightly better than they were last time. You can see what you did to overcome them, and very importantly, how good you felt after you beat them.

# Affirmations

Affirmations are short, meaningful statements that provide positive reinforcement to any desired objective that you might have. I'm sure you've seen many affirmations on posters and websites. Here are a few typical affirmations:

'Today is going to be a really good day.'

'Every day, in every way, I'm getting better and better.'

'I am confident in my own abilities.'

'Making friends comes naturally to me.'

Affirmations can be very effective when used properly. They are best when you have a very specific objective that you wish to achieve, like quitting smoking.

In order to harness the full potential of affirmations, you need to find a quiet space by yourself. It only takes a few moments.

Follow the calming breathing exercise outlined in the Introduction to the Hypnotherapy Sessions. To save you looking back for it, here it is again:

*Firstly, sit yourself down in a comfortable chair. Eventually, you'll be able to do this anywhere, but for now, make yourself comfortable. Don't cross your legs, and place your feet flat on the floor. If it's possible, take off your shoes. Cup your hands and place them palm upwards in your lap, or rest your arms on the arms of the chair.*

*Now close your eyes.*

*Sit still for a while and gently bring your attention to your breathing. Is your chest expanding as you breathe in or is it your tummy? If your chest is expanding as you breathe, then you've developed bad breathing habits. Switch your breathing so that your tummy expands and not your chest. Like a baby. This is called diaphragmatic breathing, and is the most efficient breathing method.*

*Breathe in through your nose and out through your mouth. Take a long, deep breath in through your nose. Hold it for a slow count of three then let it out through your mouth. As you exhale, let your shoulders drop and relax.*

*Breathe in again, slowly and deeply, through your nose. Hold the breath for a slow count of three, then let it go through your mouth, again allowing your shoulders to drop and relax even more.*

*Again.*

*Now return to your normal breathing pattern (but remembering to breathe diaphragmatically).*

*Feel your stresses fall away through your feet and into the ground.*

Now, once you are relaxed, you can begin making your affirmations. It's a good idea to come up with your own, but here are a few suggestions:

'I am a non-smoker. I have no wish to smoke.'

'Cigarettes damage my health. I no longer smoke.'

'<name> was being put in danger by my smoking. S/he is now safe as I no longer smoke.'

'I breathe in fresh air. I enjoy not being a smoker.'

'I am getting healthier and healthier. I love the feeling.'

'My airways are clear and clean.'

'I am smoke-free, now and forever.'

'I will remain smoke-free for the rest of my life.'

'I choose fresh air over smoke. I choose life over death.'

'I am smoke-free and my body is healing itself every day.'

'I am more attractive to other people now I am smoke-free.'

'I can do anything I want without the need to smoke.'

'Cigarette smoke is repellent. I dismiss it from my life.'

'I can control my cravings. They do not control me.'

'My desire to smoke is getting less and less every day.'

'I look great, I smell great. I am a non-smoker.'

'I can smell and taste food better and better each day.'

'I am more confident in social situations now I am smoke-free.'

'Cigarettes disgust me.'

'My world is fresher and cleaner now there is no smoke in it.'

'I am smoke-free. I am free. I am happy.'

Choose three or four affirmations that work particularly well for you (better still, make your own). Write them down on a piece of paper or on your mobile phone. Look at them often and repeat each affirmation half a dozen times or so, really listening to the words in your head as you do. Feel the truth and power of each affirmation, and let it sink deep into your subconscious, where it will do the most good.

At any point in the day, even if you're in a noisy or stressful situation, you can mutter these affirmations under your breath to yourself. Nobody will hear you and they *will* make you feel better.

The key to successful affirmations is constant repetition. Visit them many times each day. Nobody else has to know that you are doing it. Just keep it to yourself, but repeat them over and over. Make it part of your day, every day.

## Eating

As mentioned previously, some ex-smokers balloon to enormous size when they give up smoking. This is because they over-compensate. Eating is an important part of quitting, but as ever, you must always eat the ***right things.***

Avoid spicy foods for the first few days. Spicy food can enhance the craving.

Avoid sugary foods as well. Sugar enhances craving. It's a fine idea to cut down on sugar anyway.

Don't forget to have a supply of nutritious nibbles to hand to satisfy the need to have something in your mouth. Carrot sticks and celery sticks have been shown to be suitable and successful cigarette substitutes.

It may help to eat six small meals a day instead of three large ones. 'Grazing' is a term often heard in healthy-eating circles these days. Eating little and often is healthier than eating the 'three square meals a day' that people in black-and-white times recommended.

After each meal, if you can manage it, brush your teeth and enjoy the fresh, cool taste.

## Time

One of the advantages you may not have thought of but which you will now gain from being a non-smoker is that of time. How much time do you think you spend smoking? You probably think it's very little. Assuming you work indoors at a place that isn't your own house, you will legally be obliged to smoke in a special area outside dedicated to smoking.

You have to get up, put on your coat if it's cold, walk out of the building to the shelter, light up, smoke the cigarette, put it out, walk back to your desk, remove your coat and sit down again. Then there are the times when you stop on your way out to the shelter or coming back from the shelter (or both!) to have a quick chat with someone you meet.

A conservative estimate would be that you spend 10 minutes per cigarette. If you smoke 10 a day, that's 1 hour and 40 minutes every day smoking.

>    11 hours and 40 minutes per week.

If you smoke 20 per day, just one pack, that's 3 hours and 20 minutes per day or

>    23 hours and 20 minutes per week.

How anyone ever has the time to smoke 100 a day is hard to imagine!

Just think of the opportunities! A 10-a-day smoker who quits has effectively given themselves one and a half working days extra in a week!

What do you think you could do with that time? You could spend more quality time with your friends and loved ones, you could finish that project that's always been nagging at you, or you could take up a new hobby. Maybe there's something that has always piqued your interest but you've never had the time to get around to it.

Now you can. If you get really interested in your new hobby, it will be even easier to get past the cravings because you'll be distracted by your new interest.

Here are a few suggestions. Some you'll scoff at – that's alright. Maybe one or two will catch your attention. Whatever makes you curious, go for it!

Reading. There are so many books on so many subjects that you cannot fail to find something to interest you. Visiting a library or bookshop is a great way to pass the time during the early days of your quitting. Just go with whatever interests you. It may lead to a lifetime's passion.

Writing. In a recent survey, people from all walks of life were asked several questions, including 'what would be your ideal job?' More people answered 'writer' than any other single occupation. What is it about writing that so many people would like to be writers? There is a saying that 'there's a book in everybody'. Is there a book in you? A short story? An article about something you know about? Writing is very absorbing (I'm very absorbed as I write this, I can tell you!) and is an ideal way of forgetting about other things that are bothering you.

Learn a musical instrument. Why not? The greatest musicians in the world all started off not knowing how to play their instrument. Maybe you'll never be a concert pianist or a great rock guitarist, but that doesn't matter. You'll be able to play an instrument, maybe along with others. You'll make new friends and maybe even a few fans. Got to be worth a go.

Start collecting items that interest you. Stamps, coins, postcards, shells, minerals, beer mats, clocks, antiques, jewellery, spoons, antiquities, autographs, bottle caps, beer bottle labels, pencils, calculators, pebbles, business cards, bookmarks, film memorabilia, tea cosies, dolls, teddy bears, deck chairs, world paper money, old photograph albums, antlers, cameras, glass eyes, gas masks, marbles, old bottles, hats, maps, pens, toys from your childhood, games, paperweights, playing cards, tarot cards, vinyl records, microscopes, steam engines, jumbo jets... I could go on, but you get the idea!

Crafts. Knitting, sewing, painting, crochet, doll-making, card-making, scrap book making, fretwork, carpentry...

Puzzles. Crosswords, sudoku, jigsaws, patience (many versions), logic problems, word-search, codebreaker... there are magazines full to bursting with these puzzles. They're a real time absorber!

Dancing. Classes are available all over the place – ballroom, waltz, tango, flamenco, disco, swing, mambo, rumba, cha cha, bolero, jive, samba, Charleston, lindy hop, jitterbug, foxtrot, quickstep, break dancing, body popping... etc.

Fishing. There's nothing like getting out into the fresh air and sitting contemplatively by the side of a river or a lake. You could try coarse angling or fly fishing. Your first fishing equipment doesn't have to be expensive, you could get some kit second hand or borrow from a friend. You may well really enjoy it.

Walking. Rambling, hiking, hillwalking, call it what you will, walking is one of the very best ways of getting the exercise that you need. You don't have to buy expensive gear (though if you intend to go walking a lot, good boots are essential). I very strongly recommend walking as a way of getting past your initial withdrawal symptoms. It may not be easy to start with – you may feel tired and breathless – but as your body begins to heal itself of the damage done by the smoke, this will become easier and easier. Going for a walk is a very good way of gauging how far you have come in your recovery. The walk that you performed easily today was the one that you struggled with last week. You will grow stronger daily. As long as you are otherwise relatively healthy (and please get your doctor's advice before starting any new exercise regime) I recommend you start by walking one mile per day. Simply walk out of your front door, keep walking for half a mile, then turn round and come home again. For most people, half a mile is about one thousand steps. One thousand out, one thousand back. That's a pretty painless way to rapidly increase your recovery rate. Breathe deeply as you walk, taking in lots of good fresh air. In a month or two, increase this to two miles per day. It should only take about 40 minutes of your time, and the benefits are simply staggering.

That's all the advice I have for you on this, your first day as a non-smoker. I wish you the very best of luck for the first 24 hours, and then the few days after that when things might be a little difficult.

If you follow the advice I have given here and in the previous sessions, and you're firm with yourself, then your ***success is virtually guaranteed***.

I would suggest that you re-read this section several times during your first couple of weeks as an ex-smoker. It will help to reinforce the fact that what you are feeling is perfectly normal. Your problems have been faced – and defeated – by millions of successful quitters before you.

Remember to listen to the hypnotherapy recording **every day**. Listen to the two-minute recording whenever the cravings become a bit too much. It will help a great deal.

When you begin to feel the cravings ebb – and this will only take a few days, then you'll be ready to move on to the next session: Remaining a Non-Smoker.

I'll see you then…

# 5

# Session 5: Remaining a Non-Smoker

If you've made it this far then you deserve very serious congratulations.

**WELL DONE!**

**You are an ex-smoker!**

**You are a non-smoker!**

We now need to make sure that you remain that way, and that you don't slide back into bad old habits. Where you are now, you know that if you were to fall back into those habits, you would really regret it, and that one day, when you're a bit older and a bit sicker, you'll have to try to give up again. Don't let that happen. You've proved to yourself and to everybody else that you are stronger than that. Remaining strong is the key to the future – or at least, to the *near* future.

Ultimately, of course, your desire to smoke will be gone forever, never to show its weaselly little face again. At this stage, however, you are probably still experiencing some desire for a smoke. It's not as strong as it was in the beginning, and it doesn't come over you as often as it did to start with.

Just think about what that means for a moment. The strength of your desire for a cigarette has been falling for a while now. **It will continue to do so.** Every day, the desire will grow weaker and weaker until it has gone completely.

Now, you are past the worst. You beat the cravings on the first day – and they were the worst. You beat them on the second day – and they were **BAD**. You beat them on the third and succeeding days. Now they're not as bad. If you could beat them on the first, second and third days, you can do so today. And if you can do it today, it will be easier tomorrow and so much easier next week. You are on a winning streak!

The waves of desire came thick and fast over the first few days, but now they're slowing down a bit. Day by day they will get slower and less frequent. So, if you can resist the number of waves of desire that came over you to start with, then you can easily overcome them as they become less frequent and weaker.

Now this may well sound trite and wishy-washy to you, and to an extent it is, but I make no apology for that – *because it's TRUE!*

The cravings *really are* getting weaker, they *really are* getting less frequent and it *really is* getting easier. Obvious, maybe, but it's important to recognise and take onboard.

# Once an Addict, Always an Addict

You are now a non-smoker, but you should always remember that *a non-smoker never smokes, ever.*

As is the case with other addicts – drugs, alcohol or whatever, once you have given up your nicotine addiction, you have given it up for good. You *cannot* just have 'one puff' for old times' sake. You can *never* have another cigarette 'just to be sociable'.

As with drug addicts and alcoholics, one little slip can lead to a full resumption of the destructive behaviour that you have worked so hard to eliminate.

In the early days of your being a non-smoker, practise saying 'no' to the offer of a cigarette. You can ask your partner or a friend to ask you quite casually at intervals during the day 'Do you want a cigarette?'

They won't actually have a cigarette for you, of course, but this is still good practice. Practise the polite refusal. 'No, thank you. I don't smoke.'

Each time you say this, feel pleased with yourself, and know that you have spoken the truth.

Back in the real world, if someone genuinely offers you a cigarette, use the same phrase. If it's someone who already knows that you have quit, refuse the cigarette and then try to work out *why* that person would want you to resume smoking. Is it because they feel weak compared to you? Is it jealousy? Does that person want to drag you back down to their level? Why? Ask them. It may make them question their own motives, and hopefully they'll never ask again

Although they may claim that the offer was made out of a genuine desire to help you, or to make you feel better, this is almost certainly not true. Deep within them, they feel they are weaker than you, and don't like seeing anyone stronger than them.

At social functions, put some distance between you and anyone who is smoking. The smell of smoke – foul though it is – could weaken your own resolve. Don't give the beast any chance to get its dirty claws into you again. Stay away. Soon enough it will hardly bother you at all.

Be aware, however, that from time to time in the future you will think 'I could really do with a cigarette.' This can happen at any time, no matter how long it is since you've given up. Don't worry – it is not a return of your cravings. You may well notice that although the feeling is 'real', you feel somehow detached from it. It's like you are watching yourself wanting a cigarette. The real you – the watcher – doesn't really want one at all. The feeling will pass quickly.

## Trigger Situations

We've looked at Trigger Situations before, and you still have to be on your guard for these. You know best what your own triggers might be:

- When you wake up.
- Breakfast.
- With a cup of coffee.
- In the car on the way to work.
- Waiting for the bus or train to work.
- Coffee breaks at work.
- Lunch.
- When you're on the telephone.
- More coffee breaks at work.
- Driving home from work.
- Waiting for the bus or train home.
- When you get home.
- With your evening meal.
- Watching television.
- On the telephone.
- Using your computer at home.

- Just before you go to bed.

Keep your substitute items with you all the time, like healthy snacks. Also, find something to fiddle with. Part of the habit of smoking is having something in your hand. Find a substitute that works for you – a pencil, a marble, a paper clip, a cocktail stick, a coin or anything else that you want.

When you're in a Trigger Situation, fiddle with your substitute item. It will help to overcome the urge to reach for a cigarette.

Another good substitute activity is doodling. You can do this whilst watching television or when on the telephone, for example. Keep a pencil and pad by the phone at home, or next to your chair so you can just pick the pen up and doodle away. Using the telephone or watching television are natural times to want a smoke, so negate that need by doodling! Yes, I know, it doesn't completely work, but it goes part way, and soon it won't matter anyway.

## Keeping on the Straight and Narrow

That's what you've got to do. Constantly remind yourself of the reasons why you quit. It may help to re-read the first two sessions: Why Do We Smoke? and Reasons to Quit. There is enough horrible stuff in there to keep you thinking the right way.

It can be enormously helpful to have your partner gently remind you from time to time (a few times a day) why it is that you have given up. You can ask them to do this, but don't be surprised if they are reluctant.

Why? Because it will seem like nagging. Nagging evokes a response of irritation or even anger. 'Stop nagging me!' 'Yes,

I KNOW!' Tell your partner that you will accept any 'nagging' about why you gave up smoking, and that you will not be annoyed or irritated by it, but that you will accept it with good grace and thank them for it. And **do that!**

Here's the truth of the matter – you *will* find it irritating and annoying. You must bear in mind that your partner is doing this (probably against their will) for several reasons.

1. You asked them to.

2. They love you.

3. They want you to give up smoking and reap all the benefits that entails.

4. They want to spend a long and healthy life with you.

Remember this when you are told for the umpteenth time why you shouldn't light up. You love your partner, yes? They love you, too. They are trying to help, through a difficult time in your life. They are risking your irritation and anger *for your benefit*.

You must take their 'nagging' in the spirit that it was given – a genuine desire to see you a healthier person who will live a damned sight longer.

This really brings the whole 'circularity' of quitting smoking into sharp relief. You *want* to give up. Your addiction does **not** want you to give up. You ask your partner to help. Your partner may be reluctant because they know it will annoy you, but they do it anyway, because you asked them to and they love you. When they do what you ask, you are **irritated** and **annoyed**.

It's crazy. That's why you must always keep clear in your mind that you **do** want to give up – for countless reasons, and that those who are supporting you deserve not to be considered as nags and irritants. That's down to you.

The whole process of giving up and becoming smoke-free is down to you. Your loved ones and friends can help, but only **you** can give up.

### *No one can give up for you.*

The good news, of course, is that you are more than capable of doing this. You have determined that you will give up smoking and become smoke-free and a hell of a lot more healthy. That in itself is a sign of great strength. You have made a difficult decision, you have bought this book. You're not going to fail now.

Hundreds of thousands of people have given up smoking, and let's be honest, some of them must have been complete idiots. If a complete idiot can do it, then you know damn well that you can do it as well.

### *Never, ever, give up giving up.*

It's a process. A process that will last the rest of your life, but that's nothing to be scared of. Your life is full of processes. Smoking will become a less and less important process until ultimately it becomes so trivial that you don't ever think of it.

The day will come – and probably a lot sooner than you think – when you don't think about smoking at all. You will just realise, maybe as you're getting ready to go to bed, that you haven't been troubled by it all day. From that day on, you will know you are truly free. You may occasionally think about smoking, but it will be from a detached, disinterested point of view, and it will have no power over you.

# Helping Others to Quit

I cannot stress strongly enough how powerful a method of remaining a non-smoker helping others to quit is.

Your own journey from being a smoker to being a non-smoker will be highly visible to those around you. You will have told everyone that you are quitting, and maybe had to remind some of them at some point.

The smokers in your life will be particularly aware of your decision, and will be watching your progress with keen interest.

Very few smokers really, *really* want to smoke. Most of the smokers you know would probably quit if they thought they could.

When we talked about Preparing to Quit (Session 3), I suggested that you talk to ex-smokers who have successfully given up smoking. If you did this, you probably found it to be the most useful and inspiring preparation for your own quitting. Having a friend give up with you makes the whole process a great deal easier. You can support each other, maybe do things together to distract you from the cravings. When things get difficult you can talk it over and joke about it. Joking is a great way to defuse difficult situations – that's why we do it.

Once you are over the main hurdle of quitting – the first two or three weeks, and more especially the first few days – life will get much simpler for you. You'll be able to tell your friends that the quitting is going well and that you can now call yourself a non-smoker.

You may well find that some of your smoking friends start asking you questions about giving up. It's likely that they want to give up too. You should jump at the opportunity to help them. Not only will you be doing them a great favour, you'll be helping yourself to stay on the straight and narrow as well.

Humans are very competitive by nature, and by helping someone else to quit, you are also placing yourself in competition with them. That may seem counter-intuitive, but just think about it for a moment.

Think how much easier it will be to resist those urges if you have someone else literally looking over your shoulder.

'They're not going to surrender, so why should I?'

'He's no better than me, if he can do it, I can do it!'

'What will she say if I cave in? The humiliation!'

This competitive edge we all have actually encourages us to support each other, because although we compete within small, close-knit groups (like you and your quit-friend), we also compete as a small group against everyone else. We build teams, and as anyone who has ever been on a sports team will tell you, there is rivalry and competition between the individual players on a team, but when it comes to a match, they all pull together to beat the other team.

This is also what happens when you have a friend quit smoking with you. Competing against your quit-friend strengthens your resolve to succeed, and you and your friend together against the world reinforces this.

Even once you're over the worst of the cravings, helping someone else to give up smoking will produce this same internal and external competition, and both of you will benefit. In this case, however, you will already have a track record, and will be seen as the stronger. Maintaining a position of strength, even in a situation like this, is a very powerful motivator. Because your friend sees you as a strong individual who can help them, you will strive to live up to their expectations of you. In doing so, you will be far less likely to slip back into your previous bad habit.

Quitting with a friend, or helping out someone else a little way further down the line is a win-win situation. You should jump at the opportunity.

## Affirmations

Remember to keep up with your affirmations. Sometimes it can seem like a bit of a drag to be constantly repeating the same things over and over again, but it really does work.

You will very likely find that you will refine your affirmations over time. You may drop some, modify the wording of others, and bring in some new ones.

Write down your affirmations in a short list. You can do this on your phone if you like. When you drop one, for whatever reason, write the list out again, without it. Equally if you modify one, or think of another one, rewrite your list.

Revisit your list often, not only to remind yourself of your current affirmations, but to note how you've progressed with each one.

# Dealing with Slips, Trips and Backslides

I have left this part of the session until the end deliberately. I fully expect most people who are following this course will not suffer from slips, trips and backslides, and so I want this section to be apart from the rest of the session.

However, we are all human, and stuff happens.

If you do find that you have had a little failing, the first thing to do is to accept fully that this was a mistake and that it was nobody else's fault.

Then forgive yourself and move on.

Put it behind you, don't beat yourself up. Revisit your reasons for quitting, have a quick look through the first sessions of this book to remind yourself of all the hideous consequences of smoking and the much brighter future you will have as a non-smoker.

You've put in a lot of hard work to get to this stage. Don't throw it all away for the sake of a small mistake. All the reasons you had for quitting are still there. Take a deep breath and carry on.

***Never give up giving up.***

Keep saying this to yourself. Use your slip as a further motivator. Turn it round to a positive.

***I slipped up once, but now I'm stronger than ever, and even more determined to quit smoking. I deserve a smoke-free life, and that's exactly what I'm going to get.***

# 6

# Session 6: Repairing the Damage

Ideally, you should read this final session once you are confident of your success. This may be several weeks after you stub out your last cigarette. If you're reading this earlier than that, then that's fine, but come back to it again a little further down the line.

As you know (it was probably one of your major reasons for giving up in the first place), cigarette smoke does terrible damage to the human body. It is very likely that if you've been a smoker for any length of time at all, there will be some damage to you.

Giving up smoking is the best thing that you could possibly do, but we are left with the previously-inflicted damage, and we're going to have to deal with that now.

Way back in Session 2, we looked at a timeline of how the body recovers after giving up smoking. Let's look at that again for a moment.

**20 minutes** after you stop smoking, your blood pressure and heart rate will decrease.

**12 hours** after you quit smoking, the levels of carbon dioxide in your blood will return to normal levels. This means that more oxygen is being processed by your lungs and is being sent via the bloodstream to your vital organs.

**3 days** after quitting, the tension eases in your bronchial tubes, and they relax, allowing you to breathe more freely.

**14 days** after you quit smoking, you will experience an increase in circulation and an improvement in lung function. Oxygen levels are returning to normal. Your heart is starting to recover, as is your liver, kidneys, brain and all the other organs.

**1 month to 9 months** after you quit, shortness of breath, coughing and mucus build-up will decrease. The scavenger cells in your lungs also return to their proper efficiency.

**2 months** after quitting, your breathing and circulation have improved markedly – your lungs are working 30% better than they were when you smoked. You are finding it easier to walk.

**1 year** after quitting, your risk of coronary heart disease will be **half** what it was when you were smoking. It may take this long for your tiredness, shortness of breath and coughing to stop completely, but it could take a lot less.

**2 years** down the road, and your risk of having a heart attack drops to close to that of someone who has never smoked. By now you are so much fitter and healthier than you were just two short years ago. The changes have been dramatic.

**5 years** after you stop smoking, **your chances of having a stroke will be reduced to the same level as a non-smoker.** Your risk of getting lung cancer has halved, and the chances of developing the other cancers associated with smoking have **dramatically reduced.**

**15 years** after you quit smoking, your chances of developing coronary heart disease are the same as those of a non-smoker. Your body is now completely free of the effects of your former addiction, and your health is equivalent to that of somebody who has never smoked.

This timeline is, of course, only a guide. If you have been a long-term heavy smoker, things may take a little longer. If you were a light occasional smoker then you may recover faster.

In either event, it is possible to accelerate the healing process by adopting a few relatively simple strategies.

Let's have a look at different aspects of smoking damage and what we can do about them.

# Clean Air

There's no getting over the fact that the lungs and pulmonary system suffer a great deal of damage from smoking. However, the good news is that the respiratory system is one of the most resilient parts of the body, and also one of the fastest to recover.

So efficient is the recovery, that excluding any complications, the lungs' capacity can be back to normal just a few days after you quit.

There are ways to maximise the health of your lungs and ensure that they are in the best condition that you can get them.

- Deep Breathing. Yes, it sounds daft to talk about the importance of breathing – of course breathing is important – but as mentioned in Session 4: Quitting, there's a right way and a wrong way. ***Diaphragmatic breathing*** is best. Refer back to the Introduction to the Hypnotherapy Sessions for the full details, but it's basically 'stomach breathing', like a baby. Breathing in a deep, cyclic manner (slowly, in through the nose, out through the mouth) a few times a day draws extra oxygen into the lungs, boosting the blood's supply of oxygen, and facilitating faster healing. Deep breathing can be done almost any time, almost anywhere. You don't have to stop what you're doing to concentrate on it, and you don't have to make a big fuss, so nobody needs to know what you're doing. Just breathe gently in through your nose and out through your mouth. Not only is it super-oxygenating your blood and healing your body, it's also a great stress-buster.

- Make your house a well-oxygenated, clean-air refuge. You must not allow visitors to smoke in your house. That is a **HUGE** no-no! Firstly, it will present a temptation that you **really** don't need. Secondly, anyone living in your house (including you) will be suffering the effects of second-hand smoke and thirdly, you're trying to get your house smelling nice, right? You don't need someone else filling it with horrible smoke smells now you've given up! ***This goes for your car as well.***

- **Houseplants.** It is almost **unbelievable** what well-chosen houseplants can do for the quality of the air in your house. Houseplants absorb carbon dioxide and release oxygen. They remove toxic pollutants from the air and neutralize them. Very importantly for your recovery, they clean the air of potential irritants to your respiratory system. They add colour and beauty to any room you put them in. They also help to de-stress you. I mean, why *wouldn't* you have a few houseplants around? The benefits of houseplants are almost too numerous to count – not only to the recovering smoker – and it makes so much sense to have some around the house that it's really difficult to think of a reason **not** to have some. Here is a list of twelve of the best houseplants for improving the quality of the air you breathe:

1. **Aloe Vera**

Removes benzene and formaldehyde.

*Aloe Vera*

**2. Bamboo Palm**

Removes benzene, formaldehyde and trichloroethylene (TCE).

**3. Barberton Daisy** (*Gerbara jamesonii*)

Removes TCE.

**4. Broadleaf Lady Palm** (*Rhapsis excelsa*)

Removes ammonia.

**5. Chinese Evergreen** (*Aglaonema modestum*)

Removes benzene and formaldehyde.

**6. English Ivy** (*Hedera helix*)

Removes airborne faecal matter particles. Put one in your loo or bathroom!

*English Ivy*


7. **Mother-in-Law's Tongue** (also known as Snake Plant) (*Sansevierra*)

Removes xylene, formaldehyde, TCE, toluene and benzene. Releases oxygen at night. Great for the bedroom.

*Mother-in-Law's Tongue*


8. **Orchids**

Release oxygen at night, so they are good to have in the bedroom. Orchids have a bit of a reputation for being hard to look after. This usually refers to being able to get them to flower rather than simply keeping them alive. Remember it's the leaves that do all the hard work, the flowers are just a bonus. Orchids come in many different types and some are very exotic and temperamental, but some varieties are much easier than others. Ask for advice at your garden centre.

*Orchids*

### 9. Peace Lily (S*pathiphyllum*)

Removes ammonia, benzene, TCE and formaldehyde.

### 10. Red-edged Dracaena (*Dracaena marginata*)

Removes formaldehyde and benzene.

*Red-edged Dracaena*

## 11. Spider Plant (*Chlorophytum comosum*)

Removes carbon monoxide, xylene and formaldehyde.

*Spider Plant*

## 12. Weeping Fig (*Ficus benjamina*)

Removes formaldehyde, xylene and toluene.

These are all very popular household plants, and you should have no difficulty in finding them. A visit to your local garden centre, plant nursery or even supermarket can be a truly eye-opening experience. If you already have plants in the house, you'll find these no harder to look after than any others – in fact, so common are these plants that you probably have some of them already.

If you're new to indoor plants, you'll be amazed at what a difference they can make to your home environment. Do pay attention to the brief care instructions that come with them, and your plants will stay with you for many, many years.

Caring for your plants and ultimately cultivating them could even become one of your new, post-smoking interests, and a trip to the garden centre is a really useful and distracting way to spend your Quitting Day or one of the difficult days that follow.

- **Air Fresheners.** Have a good think about this one. If you have an air freshener in the house at the moment, just have a look at the list of ingredients. Do you know what any of them are? Air fresheners are full of chemicals, most of which you haven't a clue about. Just how safe are they? Are any of those chemicals likely to trigger allergic reactions? You don't know – of course you don't. The fact is that a clean, well-ventilated house should not need artificial air fresheners. If your house really does need air fresheners, try to find out why. What is causing your air to be stale or smelly? There will be an underlying problem that may need fixing. I know that animals can be a source of unwanted smells, and I'm not suggesting getting rid of your beloved pets, but maybe Bonzo could do with an occasional bath! Yes, I know, he'll hate it.

- **Herbal Remedies for the Respiratory System.** With the advice of a pharmacist or a health-food specialist, look for herbal remedies that contain the following – flavonoids, antioxidants, vitamins A, B12, C, zinc and iron. Flavonoids are the chemicals responsible for giving fruit and vegetables bright colours. This is why it's recommended to eat brightly coloured vegetables like peppers, tomatoes and so on. See below for a more detailed discussion on healthy eating.

- **House cleaning products:** Check the ingredients of the products that you use when cleaning the house, such as bathroom cleaners, floor wax, furniture polish etc. Check for irritants, and try to find products that don't contain them. Some cleaning products do need harsh chemicals in them, or they simply won't work, so when you're using them, be aware of potential irritation to your skin and lungs, and act accordingly.

# Diet

Horrible word, isn't it? It conjures up images of misery and starvation, and weeks and weeks of self-denial and lack of fun.

It needn't be like that. A few lifestyle changes – and they don't have to be big changes – and you can drastically improve your health and prospects for the future.

We'll start with some fairly easy steps. Firstly, cut down on caffeine. Caffeine occurs in many foodstuffs, though most people would immediately think of coffee. One teaspoon of instant coffee contains (depending on the roast) about 30-40mg of caffeine, which means that a normal mug of coffee contains on average about 72mg of caffeine. A strong coffee, like an espresso, may contain over 200mg of caffeine per cup.

Coffee from high street coffee shops can be considerably higher in caffeine, studies recording up to 475mg in a 20 oz cup of Starbucks Blonde Roast (*Source: US Center for Science in the Public Interest*).

The concentration of caffeine in tea is actually higher than in coffee, but as tea is served in a far more diluted form, a cup of tea will have about half the caffeine of a cup of coffee. This will be dependent on how strongly it is brewed. A weak cup of tea will have about 20mg of caffeine, a strong brew about 40mg.

Chocolate also has caffeine in it. A 50g bar of dark chocolate has up to 50mg of caffeine, a 50g bar of milk chocolate up to 25mg.

Other foodstuffs also contain caffeine. If you're a fan of those chocolate-covered coffee beans, then beware! 100g of chocolate-coated coffee beans contains up to ***900mg of caffeine***! A standard serving (30–40g), therefore, contains about 300mg of caffeine.

You should also beware of canned soft drinks. Many of these have high levels of caffeine in them, especially energy drinks. At this stage in your recovery, you need to read the labels on cans to see which drinks are acceptable, and which are going to cause you problems.

**What is the problem with caffeine, anyway?**

It's addictive. It can be *very* addictive, and it can lead to serious health issues. I think we're all aware that having too much coffee can lead to 'jitters'. This is the first sign of problems. Nausea, constant rushing to the loo, nervousness and sleeplessness are signs that you're taking too much caffeine in.

**What is the safe limit?**

Most researchers are in agreement that about 400mg of caffeine per day is probably safe. For pregnant women, however, this should be reduced to 200mg.

400mg is four or five cups of coffee per day.

That is *safe.* However, it may be too much if you are in the delicate early days of nicotine withdrawal. Your nicotine withdrawal produces symptoms very much the same as those caused by too much caffeine, and you really don't want to be making that any worse than it is.

> *Too much caffeine will make giving up tobacco much harder.*

You should consider cutting down on your caffeine intake while you get over the nicotine. Fortunately, decaffeinated coffee is easily obtained, and tastes exactly the same as normal coffee. For comparison, a normal cup of coffee contains about 72mg of caffeine, a cup of decaf contains about 1mg.

Decaffeinated tea is also widely available, and has even less caffeine in it than decaffeinated coffee.

You should also increase the amount of plain water that you drink. Water is an excellent detoxifier. It literally washes the toxins out of your system. A general recommendation is that you drink about six glasses of water per day.

I'll clear up a common mistake here. You see that 'six glasses a day' recommendation everywhere. It's a bit misleading. The body requires the equivalent of six glasses of water per day, that is certainly true, but it actually gets most of this through the food that you eat.

However, if you stick to the 'six glasses' rule, you'll be doing yourself a favour, because the extra water speeds up the flushing out of the toxins from your body. It will do you no harm at all and probably a great deal of good – and it's easy.

Fruit juice may provide more 'interest' than plain water. It also provides vitamin C, otherwise known as ascorbic acid. Vitamin C is a substance that we cannot retain in our bodies, and so we need to take some every day.

We need about 40mg of vitamin C per day, and most people will consume about 80mg through a normal, healthy diet.

A diet that consists largely of processed food and fast food may be deficient in vitamin C. Eating a healthy amount of fruit and veg every day will keep your vitamin C levels at the right level.

Vitamin C helps in the healing of wounds – in fact, one of the symptoms of vitamin C deficiency is that wounds don't heal well, or reopen once they seem to have healed.

It also helps in the elimination of free radicals. Free radicals are molecules that exist in the body's cells, which have been found to cause damage to those cells, resulting in many diseases and illnesses such as cancer.

The class of molecules which combat these free radicals are called antioxidants and vitamin C is one of these.

## Foods to Avoid

It is undeniable that our population as a whole is growing more unhealthy. Obesity is becoming a serious problem, even amongst children. The reason for this isn't hard to find. The huge increase in obesity and related poor health can be put down to the way we eat, and the way we exercise.

The increase in convenience food and fast food over the past few decades has made us lazy. It's so easy to buy food ready-made from a popular fast food outlet, or to stick a frozen something in the microwave.

The problem is that these easy solutions bring with them a whole host of problems. Fast food is usually fried or deep-fried. This is the worst possible way to prepare food from a health point of view. The food is literally saturated in fat.

Fast food, in addition to being very fatty, also very often has way too much sugar and way too much salt. **Fat, sugar and salt are the evil trinity of nutrition**, and you should work to cut these three elements right down. Don't attempt to eliminate them entirely from your diet. All three are essential to life, but in much, much smaller quantities than most people consume them.

Let's put this into perspective. **The** most important factor in regard to your health is whether you smoke or not. This is the most important factor, bar none. Now you've rid yourself of that particular evil, the next most important factor in your health is your **weight**.

This is why it is vital that when giving up smoking, you don't resort to over-eating. It can happen, very easily.

The best way for you now to repair the damage that your previous smoking has done, and to ensure a happier, healthier life for the future, is to examine your diet and make any appropriate changes.

I don't know how many times you eat food from a fast food outlet. Maybe you never do – great, you're doing yourself a great favour. Most of us, however, will have seen TV programmes where families are highlighted who literally have fast food for **every** meal. As a rule, these families are overweight and of poor health, and no wonder.

**Fast food should really be treated in the same way as smoking. It's bad for your health, it's expensive, and it's provided by companies that want your money and care nothing for your health. Oh yes, and** *people do die from eating too much fast food*.

If you're a fast food junkie, you should give very serious thought to cutting down. Make your trip to the fast food outlet a treat instead of a daily occurrence. Ease yourself away from it gradually. It's much easier to give up fast food than it is to give up smoking, and you've managed that. Cut it down first to a couple of times a week, then down to once a week. Then try a full week without.

If you do this and replace your convenience foods with healthy, home-made foods, you will eventually have a revelation.

I speak from experience here. I know it's true because it happened to me and it happened to several other people I know who cut out convenience food.

The revelation is this: ***Fast food is horrible***.

Really, seriously. Once you've weaned yourself off excess fat, salt and sugar, if you have a quick burger-in-a-bun or something out of a bucket (the fast food companies really are taking the proverbial here, making you eat out of a flaming *bucket, like a pig*), you will realise just how fatty, salty and really unpleasant it is. And what a revelation that is!

I'm not going to go into great detail here. If you want the full scary facts, an internet search should provide you with plenty. Use searches like 'problems with fast food', 'diseases caused by junk food', 'harmful effects of sugar', 'harmful effects of fat', 'harmful effects of salt' and so on.

The problems associated with bad eating are so similar to the problems with smoking that I had a real sense of *deja-vu* when I was researching this section. Here's a familiar list:

- Cancer – many varieties, including cervical, colon, gall-bladder, kidney, liver, ovarian, uterine, and post-menopausal breast cancers.

- Heart disease

- High blood pressure

- Stroke

...and to those you can add diabetes and osteoporosis. Type 2 diabetes is particularly on the increase at the moment – so much so that it is being treated as an epidemic.

We've been here before, haven't we?

### *What's the alternative?*

The alternative is to adopt a healthy eating plan. Cut out fast food (rightly called 'junk food', as it fills you up without providing anywhere near enough nutrition), cut right down on processed food, watch your sugar and salt intake.

The great news is that eating fresh, home cooked food is one of life's greatest pleasures. There are countless recipe books available which focus on healthy eating, and many of the recipes are surprisingly simple – even I can make these dishes, and that's really saying something!

The recommendation is that you eat five or more portions of fruit and vegetables during a day. The emphasis should be on vegetables rather than fruit, so more veg than fruit. In this case, a 'portion' is 80 grammes. That isn't a huge amount, a little less than 3oz. In a day, then, you should be aiming at eating about 400g or 15oz (or more) of vegetables and fruit.

There are so many ways to cook your veg. Stir-fries, curries, tagines, all remarkably simple to do and utterly fantastic.

The healthiest way to prepare your vegetables is to steam them. This can be done easily in a microwave oven, either in a microwave steamer (these are very inexpensive) or in microwave steamer bags. Either way, you'll have your veg in the best possible condition.

If you're a meat eater, you don't have to cut meat out, either. However, it's a good idea to shift away from red meats and onto white meats. White meats are those with very little fat in them.

Red meats are: Beef, pork, lamb, mutton etc.

White meats are: Chicken, turkey, ostrich, venison etc.

Yes, even though venison looks about as red as it can get, it is actually so very low in fat that it is sometimes classed as a white meat. It is also packed with vitamins, and eaten in moderation is actually good for you!

Store fresh vegetables and meat in your freezer, so they're ready any time you want them. If you find a particularly good recipe, make a big batch and store it in portion-sized containers in the freezer. Now that's Real Food – Fast!

The spices used in curries are packed with healthy compounds. We'll look quickly at just one of the spices very often found in curries – turmeric.

Turmeric is the spice that gives curry its yellow colour. It contains a very important compound called curcumin, and several very similar compounds, collectively called curcuminoids. Curcumin is a natural anti-inflammatory and antioxidant which not only fights free radicals (see above) on its own, but also stimulates the body to generate its own antioxidant enzymes.

Curcumin has also had reported benefits in the prevention and treatment of heart disease, cancer, brain diseases, Alzheimer's disease, arthritis, depression and several other chronic illnesses. What's not to love about your curry now?

In all honesty, the amount of curcumin you will get from the couple of teaspoons of turmeric in your curry is quite low, but curcumin supplements can be bought which provide a medically significant dosage. It's advised that if you do buy curcumin supplements, you should choose one that contains piperine (also known as bioperine), the chemical responsible for the smell of black pepper. Piperine works as a 'go-between' between your body and the curcumin, allowing the body to absorb and use most of the curcumin. Without this peppery intervention, most of the curcumin will simply pass through your body.

Other easy changes include drinking more healthy beverages, like green tea, or even better, white tea. White tea is the least-processed tea (your normal teabag contains black tea, which has been fermented). Any tea is good for you, and full of health-giving compounds, but white tea is the best of all. The benefits of drinking white tea are remarkable. Its flavour is less intense and more delicate than the black tea you're probably used to, so it should be drunk without milk.

Here are just a few of the recognised benefits of drinking white tea:

- It's a great source of antioxidants
- It's a cancer preventative
- It improves oral health generally
- It has anti-ageing properties
- It helps to prevent heart disease
- It's an antibacterial agent

- It provides chemicals vital for good skin
- It helps to control diabetes
- It has been reported that it helps in weight-loss AND
- It's a cure for the common cold (well alright, not quite, but it does provide relief from the symptoms of the common cold).

All this from a quick brew! White tea is available in loose leaf form or in teabags. Either way, it's a total no-brainer!

Space prevents me from going into any great detail on healthy diets here, but there are hundreds of thousands of books and interesting websites out there to help you.

## Exercise

Combined with a healthy diet, a small amount of regular exercise is the key to a long and healthy life. You don't have to join a gym and pump weights for hours at a time, either.

There are four basic types of exercise – ***aerobic, strength, flexibility*** *and* ***balance.***

For the purposes of this session, we're going to concentrate mostly on aerobic exercise. This is sometimes called 'endurance' exercise, and is designed to get your heart working harder than normal, which strengthens it and also gets highly oxygenated blood rushing round your body, nourishing and repairing all your organs.

The NHS Choices website, which can be found at

https://www.nhs.uk/Livewell/fitness/Pages/physical-activity-guidelines-for-adults.aspx

recommends that you perform 150 minutes moderate aerobic activity per week. They give the following examples of moderate aerobic activity:

- Brisk walking
- Water aerobics
- Riding a bike on level ground with few hills
- Doubles tennis
- Pushing a lawn mower
- Hiking
- Skateboarding
- Rollerblading
- Volleyball
- Basketball

If you prefer, you can substitute the 150 minutes of moderate aerobic exercise with 75 minutes of vigorous exercise. This would be activities such as:

- Jogging, running
- Fast swimming
- Riding a bike fast, or over hills
- Singles tennis
- Football
- Rugby
- Skipping rope
- Hockey
- Gymnastics
- Martial arts

As well as this activity, you should also do some strengthening exercises such as:

- Weight lifting
- Working with resistance bands
- Press-ups, sit-ups
- Digging in the garden
- Yoga

on at least two days per week.

You should choose an activity that suits you best. It might be worth trying a few different ones out before deciding which one (or which ones) you're going to stick with.

My personal choice is walking. For me, it's simply the easiest choice. You don't need to buy any special kit (though a good pair of walking boots will prove to be a very sound investment). You just step out of the front door of your house and off you go!

Note that the walking should be ***brisk***. Just gentle strolling will not give anywhere near the benefits that brisk walking will provide. What, exactly, do I mean by **brisk walking**?

Walking is 'brisk' when you find yourself breathing through your mouth rather than your nose. You don't simply breathe through your mouth, but allow your body to tell you when it's time to start bringing more oxygen in to sustain your hard-working muscles.

Another way to look at it is to say that you are walking briskly when you can talk, but you can't sing. If you **can't talk**, you're going too quickly. If you **can sing**, you're going too slowly.

If you are reasonably healthy – and remember if you've just given up smoking, you probably won't be – then at a reasonably brisk pace, you should be able to walk one mile in about

15 to 20 minutes. 15 minutes is quite fast, and would more likely be achieved by someone with longer legs.

A two-mile walk will therefore take you between 30 and 40 minutes. That's about right, and you should aim to be able to do no less than two miles when you go for your walk.

If you find that a struggle in the early stages of quitting, start with one mile.

As a rough rule of thumb, a mile is about 2000 footsteps. You can count these as you go along. A simple method of remembering where you're up to is to hold a different finger for each hundred that you reach. When you reach 100 steps, hold your thumb with your forefinger. At 200 steps, hold your forefinger with your thumb, at 300 steps hold your middle finger with your thumb, and so on. Once you reach 600 steps, switch to your other hand and hold that thumb with that hand's forefinger.

To walk two miles, set off from your house for 2000 footsteps then turn round and come back again by the same route. Easy peasy.

Better still, find a nice circular route and measure it out by counting paces.

Do your two miles five times a week, and **never** avoid it. It's half an hour, time that is *entirely yours*, nobody pressuring you, all problems left behind, and it's actively making you healthier.

**After actually quitting, exercise is the single most important factor in repairing the damage that has been done to your body and restoring your health. Do NOT ignore this!**

There are so many people out there, already walking for their own health or walking dogs that you will probably even make some new friends!

## Cleaning Yellow-Stained Fingers

The tar in cigarettes leaves unsightly staining on your teeth, gums and fingers. Fortunately, there are inexpensive ways to remedy this.

The first method you can use to clean your fingers and nails is to soak them in lemon juice. Lemon juice is a great stain remover. Dip your fingers in a bowl or cup of lemon juice for a few minutes then rub them with a flannel. If the flannel is not harsh enough, try a nail file or a pumice stone. Only rub gently. It may take a few sessions doing this before your fingers are completely clear of the staining.

A second method involves you making your own scrubbing paste. Mix 50g of baking soda with 100g of hydrogen peroxide, making a smooth paste. Soak your fingers in this paste for 10 minutes or so, and repeat daily until the stains have gone.

You can also use nail varnish remover (acetone) on a cotton wool ball to wipe the stains away, but as acetone is an irritant if inhaled, do be careful!

## Cleaning Yellow-Stained Teeth

A trip to the dentist may be in order initially, to get a good cleaning done. You can, however, use the same baking soda and hydrogen peroxide paste as a toothpaste. Hydrogen peroxide can be harmful if swallowed in sufficient quantity, so make sure firstly that you're using a well-diluted solution. Don't swallow it and rinse your mouth out thoroughly afterwards.

# Finally

We've now reached the end of our journey together. It's been a tough one, with many ups and downs. By the time you reach this penultimate page, you should be well on your way to being a forever non-smoker.

The cravings for nicotine should now have reduced to a quite ignorable little nag, and soon even that will be gone. You've started on a new phase of your life, when your health is now improving rather than plummeting downwards.

If you've got this far and managed to remain smoke-free, I want to congratulate you. You are a **fighter**, a **winner**, a **STAR**! You are a *happier, healthier you* than you were when you started reading this book. All that remains is for me to thank you for allowing me to accompany you during this momentous time in your life and to wish you all the very best for the future, and to welcome you to the ever-growing number of non-smokers.

# Appendix

## Internet resources

*Quit! Website: the website for this book:*

https://quitsmokebook.com

*Get your FREE hypnotherapy sessions here:*

https://quitsmokebook.com/hypnosessions

*NHS Choices:*

https://www.nhs.uk/live-well/quit-smoking/

*Physical activity guidelines:*

https://www.nhs.uk/live-well/exercise//

*Exploding vape pen kills man in Florida – Daily Mail:*

https://www.dailymail.co.uk/news/article-5735287/TV-producer-killed-vaping-pen-explodes-penetrating-brain.html

## One last thing...

Getting this book out into the world where it can do some good is very important to me. If you have found this book and hypnotherapy recordings helpful in your own battle against the beast, I would *really* appreciate some positive feedback from you. Please go to Amazon and review this book.

If you wish to contact me, please send an email to:

quitsmoking.paulmetcalfe@gmail.com

I would love to read your success stories, suggestions and questions. If you need additional one-on-one mentoring to help you quit for good, I would be delighted to help you by phone or video call. Email me for details.

Thank you.

# Index

## A

addiction, 15, 30, 35, 72, 78, 87, 108
Aloe Vera, 118
Alzheimer's, 131
American Cancer Society, 52
ammonia, 20, 119
antioxidants, 55, 57, 123, 126, 131

## B

Bamboo Palm, 119
Barberton Daisy, 119
benzene, 20, 119, 121
blood pressure, 21, 40, 115, 129
breathing, 42, 89, 96, 116, 117
Broadleaf Lady Palm, 119

## C

caffeine, 124
carbon monoxide, 20, 21, 122
cash, 38, 51, 93
Chinese Evergreen, 119
curcumin, 130

## D

diet, 124, 132

## E

eating, 79, 98, 123
e-cigarettes, 72
English Ivy, 119
exercise, 81, 89, 101, 127, 132

## F

fast food, 126, 128, 129
fat, 127
formaldehyde, 20, 119, 121
free radicals, 126, 130

## H

heart, 21, 40, 42, 44, 116, 129, 131, 132
herbal remedies, 123
house cleaning products, 123
hydrogen cyanide, 20, 42
hydrogen sulphide, 20
hypnotherapy, 8, 11

## M

Mother-in-Law's Tongue, 120

## N

NHS, 84, 132
nicotine, 15, 19, 22, 25, 34, 70, 78, 87, 90

## O

orchids, 120

## P

Peace Lily, 121
pregnancy, 17, 55

## R

Red-edged Dracaena, 121

## S

salt, 127, 129
sexual problems, 39, 57
skin, 22, 38, 47, 123, 132
Snake Plant, 120
Spider Plant, 122
S-T-A-R-T strategy, 68
stress, 19, 27, 34, 38, 45, 69, 71, 74
substitute behaviour, 29

sugar, 29, 79, 98, 127, 129

## T

trigger situations, 106
turmeric, 130

## V

vaping, 71, 72
vitamin C, 126

## W

walking, 134
Weeping Fig, 122
white tea, 131
withdrawal, 16, 19, 25, 34, 78, 80, 90

## Y

yellow-stained fingers, 136
yellow-stained teeth, 136

Printed in Poland
by Amazon Fulfillment
Poland Sp. z o.o., Wrocław